FOCUS ON THE FAMILY

W9-BYP-570

A N S W E R I N G
THE CALL

SAVING INNOCENT LIVES, ONE WOMAN AT A TIME

J O H N   E N S O R

Answering the Call
Copyright © 2003 by John Ensor
All rights reserved. International copyright secured.

ISBN: 1-58997-152-3

Published by Focus on the Family
8605 Explorer Drive
Colorado Springs, CO 80920

Focus on the Family books are available at special quantity discounts
when purchased in bulk by corporations, organizations, churches, or
groups. Special imprints, messages, and excerpts can be produced to
meet your needs. For more information, contact: Resource Sales Group,
Focus on the Family, 8605 Explorer Drive, Colorado Springs, CO
80920; or phone (800) 932-9123.

Cover Design: Kurt Birky
Cover Photo: Photodisc

Printed in the United States of America
7 8 9 / 08 07 06

To Nathanael, Megan, and Elliot,
cherished children who prove that the aroma of
life comes in three distinctly delightful fragrances

/ CONTENTS /

Contents

/ FOREWORD /

As you read this book, you will discover that John Ensor combines several very special qualities: a pastor's heart, an activist's motivation, and a Good Samaritan's compassion.

Because he previously served as a pastor, he identifies with the clergy's struggles in addressing difficult biblical issues that have become social/moral issues in our society.

Because John sees how much there is to do in reaching out to scared, hurting women facing unplanned pregnancies, he strongly encourages Christians' involvement.

Because he has seen the fear and pain these women experience (in his present role as executive director of a group of pregnancy resource centers), he approaches their need with God's love and empathy.

Will you spend a few moments with John, hearing his heart as he points us to the Father's heart on the important biblical principle of the value of all human life? I promise you'll never be the same.

Julie A. Parton, Ph.D.
Manager, Crisis Pregnancy Ministry
Focus on the Family

ONE

The Aroma of Life

A few people in King David's time provided such wise assessment of and bold influence on their generation that it became their lasting testimony. They were the "men of Issachar," and they were described as men "who understood the times and knew what Israel should do" (1 Chronicles 12:32). Recognizing the vital need for such people in every age, *Answering the Call* is designed to help Christians take the initiative in influencing our generation on a matter of great importance: cherishing and defending innocent human life.

For the past 12 years I have sought to help the Christian community understand the times in which we live, specifically at the intersection of biblical ethics and cultural conflict. I have been invited into hundreds of pulpits to address the painful and sensitive issue of abortion. It has been my unwavering hope each time to fashion a powerful, even historic, life-affirming Christian response from the church. I may fail, but I see no evidence that any other group of people is capable of taking up this burden. Throughout history, right to the present hour, it has been in large part only the Christian community that has cared enough to oppose with courage and compassion the pagan "rights" of abortion, infanticide, and euthanasia.

In the main, pastors and laypeople alike *understand* that cherishing and defending innocent human life is a moral mandate. It is the law of love. They understand that abortion is an act of violence that kills a baby and damages every mother and father.

But how to take action is often difficult to determine. The importance of speaking up for the preborn is easy to lose sight of, given all the demands on our time. And let's be honest, there is an internal bias against knowing too much about abortion or saying too much about it.

As a moral, ethical, and biblical matter, the sanctity of human life is something we uphold as a matter of creed and intellect. But the silence of our pulpits in addressing abortion indicates that as pastoral leaders, we are uncertain what to say beyond a fleeting condemnation. And for lay-people, the fact that "cherishing and defending innocent human life" is not an overt value woven into the mainstream of church ministries reflects the same timidity and ambivalence.

The apostle Paul describes the role of the church in the world to be so boldly arresting, so wooingly fragrant, that we are the very aroma of life itself (2 Corinthians 2:16). For many people I have met, the situation is more like dealing with an unseemly smell coming from the basement during a family celebration. Something is wrong, but what should one say to the hostess? First attempts may be glances toward the basement door, followed by a whisper or two privately ("Am I imagining things, or is there a problem here?"). After a while we may get used to it and forget about the matter. Still, if we love our hostess and care about the health of the family, we look for ways to deal with it. That is the position many Christians take today. They want to cherish and defend innocent human life, but they want to do it sensitively and rationally. *Answering the Call* is for them.

The need, of course, is not only to *inform* people of the divine call to cherish and defend innocent human life, but also to *inspire* God's people to life-saving and life-changing intervention on behalf of the weak and the innocent. In general, the Christian community is a life-affirming people. If they are provided a practical venue for demonstrating their concern for needy mothers and babies, they will respond enthusiastically.

Therefore I recommend that the call to cherish and defend innocent human life always be coupled with direct intervention with those in pregnancy distress. Every church in America can and should be partnering with its local crisis pregnancy centers (also called pregnancy help centers or pregnancy resource centers). While many other arenas for life-affirming action cry out for attention, this should be first on the list.

There are two reasons I suggest this. First, all

abortion is local; it befalls one woman at a time. Frightened mothers who are planning to abort their babies tomorrow are agonizing tonight in homes *in our neighborhoods*. Second, the Great Commandment calls us to love our neighbors. A woman in an unplanned pregnancy is truly frightened and feels that her very life is ending—not physically, but emotionally and spiritually; her life as she has projected it seems threatened. Strange and perverse as their end is, abortionists parrot the same message that Christ offers to those in trouble: "Come to me, all you who are weary and burdened, and I will give you rest. Take my yoke upon you…" (Matthew 11:28-29). Abortionists promise deliverance, but the "rest" they provide is death itself.

We have a special duty as the Christian community to refute the false mercy of the abortion industry, especially, and primarily, in our neighborhoods. We know the *true* Rescuer, the *true* Savior, the One who gives life and nourishes it, the One who is eminently trustworthy to provide daily bread as well as the forgiveness of sins. We, in His name, should be broadcasting in every neighborhood across the land, "Come to me, all you who are weary and burdened (by an unplanned pregnancy). Take my yoke (the way, the truth, and the life I have found in Christ) and learn from me, for Our God is gentle and humble in heart (neither harsh nor condemning) and you will find rest for your souls (I will show you the better way and you will delight in it). For His yoke is easy and His burden is light."

In practice, the best way to bring this winsome invitation to abortion-vulnerable women in our neighborhoods is to partner with local crisis pregnancy centers. Day after day, without fanfare or major funding, they provide mothers in pregnancy distress the support they need to prepare for parenting or adoption. There are more than 3,000 such centers across the country, and more opening internationally. Almost all of them are organized as Christian ministries. With a little more help, they could reach many more mothers. Dr. James Dobson, president of Focus on the Family, has urged churches and Christians to partner with their local center:

> I consider abortion to be the greatest moral
> evil of our time, because of the worth of

those little babies. At the end of the year a crisis pregnancy center can point to a baby boy, born January 12th, a baby girl, born February 22nd—real, live human beings who were allowed to live, to be brought into the world, to give love and receive love simply because those organizations exist. Crisis pregnancy centers serve the community, by serving mothers-to-be caught in the most traumatic time of their life.[1]

As the founder of five such centers, I can assure you that this is true. Even more, those churches that have broken the silence and put neighborly love into action have discovered afresh the old truism, "There is joy in serving Jesus."

/ Two /

The Great Test and the Great Work

Legal abortion, widely accepted in the culture, represents the great test before this present generation of Christians. Will we hold each life precious, as previous generations have done, and courageously and resolutely cherish and defend innocent human life? Or will we slide along with postmodernism's moral freefall? Pope John Paul II calls it a great struggle between the "gospel of life" and the "culture of death."[1] D. James Kennedy, senior pastor at Coral Ridge Presbyterian Church in Fort Lauderdale, Florida, said, "Abortion has become *the* issue in this country, for if you lose life, you lose all. If Christians do not win on this issue, we will not win on any issue."[2]

You may not yet agree. What does appear self-evident is that, as we have been warned by many over the years, *abortion has led to a general diminution of human life.* Physician-assisted suicide, cloning, embryonic stem-cell research—each has its accompanying lobby of scientists and movie stars trumpeting utopian benefits.

Peter Singer, the Ira DeCamp Professor of Bioethics at Princeton's Center for *Human Values* (italics added), advocates extending so-called abortion rights to include newborns, so that parents might be allowed to kill their babies until the child is deemed "sentient," or self-aware.[3] While not yet a, mainstream idea, infanticide is rising dramatically.

"Girl, 16, said to suffocate infant"
"Teen is charged with killing baby at prom"
"Body of baby found in ditch"

These are real newspaper headlines. According to U.S. Justice Department statistics, the rate of infanticide has doubled in the United States since abortion became legal.[4]

What about anti-child behavior that stops short of death? Statistics from the American Humane Association and the National Committee for the Prevention of Child Abuse confirm that child abuse and neglect have risen fourfold since the legalization of abortion.[5]

Utilitarian ethics, the notion that some lives can be destroyed to improve the lives of others, are extremely attractive to our narcissistic, sin-stained nature. Combating it requires Christians, gripped by the moral clarity and courage of the Son of God Himself, to "speak up for those who cannot speak for themselves" (Proverbs 31:8). In addition, it takes an army of "worker bees" reaching out and assisting those women in their neighborhoods who are in pregnancy distress. Abortion advocates are counting on our silence and inactivity. An intimidated clergy and a distracted Christian community are prerequisite for the deconstruction of the national ideal that all men are created by God and possess an inalienable right to "life, liberty, and the pursuit of happiness" (and in that order).

Therefore, legalized abortion is the great test for this generation of Christians. The great work before us is cherishing and defending innocent human life. How we do that comes down to following the Great Commandment, the law of love.

The Law of Love: What Is the Christian Thing to Do?

The law of love teaches us to love our neighbors as ourselves. The parable of the Good Samaritan illustrates the law's practical, on-site power to transform a deadly situation into a life-saving, God-exalting circumstance. The Golden Rule in Matthew 7:12 is the law of love stated another way. We are to respond to the needs of others as we would hope others would respond to our own need. This is the law of love. The human heart, when enriched with divine love, creates a life-cherishing, life-saving, life-changing dynamic of human effort and creativity.

For example, a young, sweet-voiced 16-year-old called my office, which was established to help women in pregnancy distress. A few minutes into telling her story, she said, "If I don't get an abortion, I'm going to kill myself." After a long pause she whispered, "And after I have my abortion, I know I'm going to kill myself." In that moment I understood again the anguish of an unplanned pregnancy. I saw the multidimensional power of death unleashed in abortion. A baby destroyed, a young girl's sense of self torn apart, parents over-wrought by their teenager's pregnancy; but what would they say of her suicide?[6]

This young teenager is my neighbor. What does it mean for me to love her as my neighbor? What is the Christian thing to do? What would *you* have me say and do for her that you think honors God and would make you proud of the Christian testimony presented to her by my words and actions? If I were unsure, what would the law of love compel you to say and do to help me help her?

Consider another real example. One couple came to see me with nine of their 10 children in tow. The mother was 15 weeks pregnant. They were Cambodian immigrants. The husband spoke in broken English, "I got laid off from my job. I have nine children to feed! My wife needs an abor-tion! I cannot afford another child." His wife sat quietly. Her countenance signaled that she was resigned to help her husband but clearly shaken at the thought of doing something contrary to her whole life experience and maternal nature.

What does the law of love require of me in this situation? What should I say to this couple? If I told you that I wished them well and sent them on their way, would you be pleased with me? Not likely. Prayer is certainly called for, but prayer alone is not *all* that love is capable of accomplishing in this situation.

A postgraduate student came to me, pregnant by one of her professors. She was finishing her doctorate and preparing to launch her career. It had taken years of work. Her parents had paid tens of thousands of dollars over the years in tuition bills. Now a baby threatened all her plans and hopes. She needed an abortion. This baby threatened her very life—not so much physically, but the life she had envisioned for herself and worked so hard to achieve. This baby was *killing* her desires and goals. In that sense, her abortion was an act of *self*-preservation.

The father of the baby came in with her to make sure she did not waiver on "the things *we* talked about and on what *we* had decided to do." In private she confessed that in spite of her situation, she was ambivalent about aborting her baby. She was going through with the abortion to please the father and her parents and her friends, all of whom counseled her that this was "not the time to have a baby." The problem was, she understood that she already *had* a baby. The choice now was whether to nurture or destroy her baby. After a brief conversation, she began to turn her mind away from abortion.

Now the father of the baby erupted. He yelled at me, threatened me, yelled at her and threatened her. I sat there thinking and praying, *What should I say to each of them? What is the Christian thing to do? What does the law of love require of me in this situation?* How would you have responded?

In one three-month period, the daughters of three local pastors came to our office. They were embarrassed, extremely frightened, somewhat defiant, and in one case, hurt and angered because her father had just thrown her out of the house. One woman came in so frightened that she called herself "X" because she was a senior at a local Christian college. She said, "I've lost my salvation. I know what God thinks about abortion." She was about to abort her *faith* as well as her baby.

Another couple came in, with a background of drugs and alcoholism. He could not read.

Neither of them had a job. They told me that they had been living together for 10 years. I asked them if they were married and they said yes. But then they explained: They were both married to someone else! Now a baby was on the way. I tried to hide my shock. I shook my head, thinking, *Lord, where do I begin?*

I ask myself in all of these cases, what does neighborly love require of me? Jesus said at the end of the parable of the Good Samaritan, "Go and do likewise." Do I have the kind of compassion it takes to let my plans be delayed to stave off the death of a fellow human being—my neighbor? What practical intervention does Christ and His law of love obligate me to provide those left for dead? If I needed help in doing it, what does love demand of *you*?

/ THREE /

Knowing the Times in Which We Live

To fail to understand what abortion is and to take some measure of its immediate, pervasive, even eternal power to destroy, is to misunderstand the times in which we live. America is a postabortion culture. Since 1973, when the Supreme Court set aside all state abortion restrictions, Americans have intentionally destroyed more than 40 million human beings in utero (conservatively estimated).[1]

At this time a woman would have to be about 75 years old or older to have lived through her childbearing years *without* abortion being both legal and easily accessible across the nation. For everyone younger, the right to abortion is all they know. It is the cornerstone of modernity, in which "choice" and "freedom" mean absolute autonomy from God and His laws. By now, most families in America have been directly affected by abortion. According to the Centers for Disease Control and Prevention, 43 percent of American women will undergo at least one abortion by the age of 45.[2]

In its wake, abortion is destroying the health and well-being of women. Dr. David Reardon, one of the nation's leading researchers on the effects of abortion, reports, "Half of all aborted women experience some immediate or long-term physical complications, and almost all suffer from emotional or psychological aftershocks."[3] Among our family and friends, coworkers and parishioners, abortion is leading to a host of infections and cancers, while guilt is gnawing away at their souls.[4]

Abortion destroys intimacy. Couples in pregnancy distress, having shared their feelings about why a baby was not in their best interest before the abortion, seldom talk about it afterward. The majority of couples break up subsequent to an abortion. For those that make it, abortion sows seeds of anger, bitterness, shame, and guilt into the marriage. Physical intimacy is stained with bloodguilt. The beauty and mystery of intercourse becomes "ground zero" in a horrific battle against God's procreative grace.

Abortion destroys the essence of femininity. All women are "Eve" (in Hebrew, "mother of all living"), possessing the potential ability to bear life. As one mother who aborted three times told me, "John, never, never forget that a woman is connected to her child by an umbilical cord that is not just physical, but emotional, psychological, and even spiritual. When we murder our own babies, *we* die as well."

Abortion also destroys masculinity. At the heart of what it means to be a man and not a woman is a sense of leadership in being the provider and protector of women and children. Abortion aborts this sense of responsibility. It weakens a man's self-image as a provider and protector. The spirit of chivalry, which always works in men to the honor of women, is destroyed. It is replaced with the predatory spirit that sees women as "mere equals" to compete with, subdue, and conquer.

Abortion aborts truth and reason as well. We rationalize that abortion could not really be homicide because that would make us, or the people we love who have yielded to abortion, guilty of homicide. We see ourselves as loving and caring people. We would *never* hurt an innocent child. In fact, we project a self-image that believes we would risk injury to save a child's life. Everyone I know believes he or she is the kind of person who would scream bloody murder if a man took a knife to a baby. Therefore abortion simply cannot involve the murder of a living human being. Our self-image precludes it.

This is why it took hundreds of years and a civil war to face what is now clear to everyone. The people who defended slavery saw themselves as good people who would never hurt or abuse another *person*. Therefore, their slaves must not be *persons*, or at least not "full" persons as *they* are. To admit the truth of abortion, like the truth of slavery, is painful. It will be all the more painful if one hundred years from now, when people look back on the inhumanity of abortion the way we presently look back at the inhumanity of slavery (and in our grief wonder how such moral blindness and civil injustice was allowed to stand in the first place), we find that the church did not take the *lead* in the abolition movement that is sure to strengthen with each generation to come.

Abortion in the Church

Part of the reason cherishing and defending innocent human life is not a vibrant, conscious, organized mainstream part of the church's mission today is because of our own guilt on the matter. We have aborted our own babies.

One out of every six abortions are performed on women who identify themselves as "born again" Christians.[5] With some 1.5 million women submitting to abortion each year, this equals 250,000 evangelically oriented Christians aborting annually. In another study, 31 percent of postaborted women identified themselves as Catholic.[6] Indeed, the abortion industry could not survive financially without the paying customers drawn from the church. Since 1973, Christians have committed homicide 5.6 million times. Every 20 seconds another baby is killed, and every minute and a half, a "born again" Christian adds to the fatality count.

I was shocked in 1989 to discover that fully 30 percent of the women in my own congregation were postaborted. I refer to this day of discovery, when we looked at the painful truth of abortion for the first time, as "the day God lanced a boil."

Prior to that time, it was common and acceptable for people to confess their involvement with drugs or alcohol or promiscuity or any other sin common in the city of Boston. But nary a word had ever been spoken about abortion. That was the unspeakable sin in our midst. The secrecy, the shame, the fear of discovery all worked to blackmail us into silence and to paralyze the church into inaction. How could we heed the biblical call to cherish and defend innocent human life when we had blood on our own hands?

After the silence was broken, women told me that for years, even as "born again" Christians, they thought, *What would everyone think of me if they ever learned that I aborted one of my own babies? What would they think of me if they learned that I aborted three of my babies?* Men mirrored the same fear and shame. *What would people think if they knew I paid money to have my own child destroyed?*

Cherishing and defending innocent human life requires us to face the truth about abortion. It is a painful truth to face, but the law of love demands it. As the first-century writer Plutarch said, "Medicine, to produce health, has to examine disease; and music, to create harmony, must investigate discord." A good doctor does not withhold the lance to spare the patient pain. Nor can good physicians of the human soul beg off examining the disease and discord now festering in 40 percent of the people in their own church. It is spiritual malpractice!

We must lance the boil of this guilt if we are going to produce true health and life. This is painful and difficult, but it is also purifying. And it is our duty. The biggest mistake we are making in our local churches today regarding abortion is rightly sensing its destructive power but then remaining silent to spare people hurt. Some tears are medicinal. This is a case, I assure you, where godly sorrow is cleansing. Make the cut and you will be able to say with the apostle Paul, "See what this godly sorrow has produced in you: what earnestness, what eagerness to clear yourselves, what indignation, what alarm, what longing, what concern, *what readiness to see justice done*" (2 Corinthians 7:11, italics added).

Imagine a whole church *ready to see justice done!* What resources would flow into the breaches to reinforce family and neighborhood foundations, as godly sorrow produced earnestness and eagerness, alarm and concern! What kingdom entrepreneurs and virtue capitalists would emerge! People who have been forgiven much love much! And this is the promise of the gospel. If we grieve what presently stains our consciences and paralyzes our life in Christ, then as Hebrews 9:14 says, Christ will "cleanse our consciences from acts that lead to death, so that we may serve the living God!"

One of the first things I needed to do as a pastor in calling my church body to cherish and defend innocent human life was to remind them what the gospel *is* and why it is called "good news of great joy" (Luke 2:10). I had to remind my dearest friends that Christ was given the name Jesus because "he will save his people from their sins" (Matthew 1:21). I had to start with some of my own elders.

Tom and Jane

Tom was (and is) a man of great passion and compassion. He was a solid elder. When he learned that abortion was to be addressed he grew unusually cautious and nervous. I did not pick up on why that might be. At first I thought it might be a general concern that abortion is "politics" rather than a legitimate moral issue right out of the Ten Commandments.

When I saw him sitting with his wife, Jane, following the service, and I saw her weeping and him sitting absolutely frozen, unable to offer her any comfort, the picture became clearer. I sat with them both and listened. She wept and, through her tears, haltingly told their story.

Before they were married, before they came to faith in Christ, they lived together in the "sex, drugs, and rock 'n' roll"-crazed era of the 1970s. They had left it years ago. Christ had changed their lives. Their testimony, and their love for people, was one of the main reasons our church was a haven for others struggling with various addictions. But never had they faced the truth about abortion, until that day.

"I have been so angry at Tom all these years for taking me to that abortion clinic," Jane confessed. "It has sown more bitterness in our marriage than anything else." It's not that Jane was shifting all the blame to Tom. She had died a thousand deaths in her own heart over the matter. It is just that a woman always hopes in that situation that her lover will be manly! The hope is that he will protect her rather than expose her to such an unnatural solution. Tom, instead of saying, "Honey, I love you. Our baby will be provided for. I will see to that," offered to help by escorting her to an abortionist and paying for it. Tom wept aloud, "It's my fault. Please forgive me." It was a painful time.

I went on to listen to each and every story of the men and women in my church who had personally been involved in abortion and who were willing to tell me their story. They taught me "the times in which we live," and they pointed us toward a Christian response.

Tom and Jane took the lead. On several occasions Tom talked openly about his own involvement with abortion—how it had affected him and his wife, their marriage and their souls. He called on the church to join him and his wife and others in reaching out to those in their neighborhood now facing the same temptations. At one point, however, his testimony changed. He had taken his wife for *two* abortions before they were married. Several months later, when Tom shared his story before a group of church leaders assembled to talk about cherishing and defending innocent human life, Tom's testimony changed again. He had aborted *three* of his children.

So deep and painful was the truth that God in His grace had to peel away the shame in layers over time rather than all at once. If you want to understand the times in which we live, and how abortion guilt is quenching the spirit of grace and power in our people, just ask those who have aborted to quietly seek you out.

I can think of no remedy to abortion guilt other than the Good News that Christ died for *all* our sins and paid the full price due for *each* of them.[7] There is no therapy, no steps program, no psychological cure for the guilt of abortion. Only the innocent blood of Christ can cleanse away the bloodguilt of abortion. So the truth of the matter comes full circle. Those who preach the gospel without ever mentioning abortion leave the very people most in need of the gospel to interpret their silence to mean that abortion is the unforgivable sin.

We must proclaim Good News to the guilty *while* cherishing and defending the innocent. In my case, out of the tears arose a people forgiven and set free to serve God with new vigor. They charged into the city, helping women in pregnancy distress find a home, find a job, and find help in raising the baby. They gave of themselves to ensure that each mother found the help she needed in preparing to parent or to release the baby for adoption. Christian women came alongside young new mothers, and Christian men birddogged young fathers until they captured a vision and a passion for fatherhood. They were alarmed at the consequences of what would happen if they did not. They were eager to see justice done and mercy triumph over judgment. They knew firsthand the injustice and exploitation going on in the abortion industry.

Abortion as a Youth-Oriented Business

It is important to understand that abortion is not just something people resort to because of personally embarrassing or difficult circumstances. Abortion is also a business with a full marketing plan. Twenty percent of abortions are performed on teenagers. They are targeted for abortion. In her pamphlet *Selling Teen Abortions*, Carol Everett, who once ran two lucrative abortion facilities in Texas (before becoming a Christian changed her life), recounts the deceptive way she marketed abortion to teenagers.[8] Using the public school system and the false promise of contraception, she promoted sexual activity. This, after all, is the only way to get more pregnancies and therefore sell more abortions. Asked how she did this, she writes:

> I established myself with the teens as an authority on sex. I explained to them that their parents wouldn't help them with their sexuality, but I would. I separated them from their support system, number one, and they listened to me. Second, our doctors prescribed low dose birth control pills with a high pregnancy rate knowing well that they needed to be taken very accurately at the same time every day or pregnancy would occur.
>
> This insured the teens to be my best customers as teenagers typically are not

responsible enough to follow such rigid medication guidelines on their own. I knew their sexual activity would increase from none or once a week to five or seven times a week once they were introduced to this contraception method. Then I could reach my goal—three to five abortions for each teenager between the ages of 13 and 18.

Obviously, unrepentant abortionists would deny such base motives. When I debate Planned Parenthood representatives, they constantly seek to switch the debate away from abortion to contraception and voice their desire to avoid pregnancies. Some, no doubt, naively believe their own "let's-promote-contraception-to-make-abortion-rare" mantra. But the evidence shows that contraception does *not* make abortion rare. According to the Centers for Disease Control and Prevention (CDC) and the Alan Guttmacher Institute (AGI), an organization strongly affiliated with Planned Parenthood, some 58 percent of all women seeking an abortion report that they *were* using birth control during the month that they become pregnant. The incidence of contraceptive use is even higher among women seeking repeat abortions—65 percent nationally.

Moreover, abortion itself has become a form of birth control. According to both the CDC and AGI, 50 percent of all abortions are repeat abortions. One in five women seeking abortions has aborted two or more babies previously.[9] As if to belie claims that abortions are somehow "necessary" for these women, both government and abortion industry data show that more than 93 percent of all induced abortions are done on perfectly healthy mothers with perfectly healthy babies.[10]

At the same time that they profess a desire to make abortion "rare," leading abortion advocacy groups are promoting mandatory abortion training at U.S. medical schools, increased access to abortion, and new and innovative forms of abortion such as methotrexate and RU-486. As a $450 million (minimum) annual industry in the United States, the abortion industry hardly seems intent on putting itself out of business. The industry has its own trade magazine, including a popular "marketing tips" column.[11]

Planned Parenthood alone reports $57 million in annual income to its national office, with some

$143 million originating from taxpayer dollars. In 1998, Planned Parenthood enjoyed $52 million in federal Title X funding (read: your federal tax dollars). This constitutes one-quarter of all annual Title X appropriations. According to IRS filings, Planned Parenthood reports annual income "in excess of expenditures" in the millions of dollars. Not bad for a so-called "nonprofit" organization!

The more its supporters promote contraception rather than abstinence before and virtue within marriage, the more abortions and "unplanned pregnancies" we experience. Christ told us that we would know a tree by the fruit it bears. Protestants as well as Catholics, in fact people of all faiths or none, should now admit that Pope Paul VI was accurate in his prophetic 1968 letter, *Humanae Vitae*. Widespread acceptance of contraception has fueled rampant nonmarital sexual activity, radically higher divorce rates, the use of women as sex objects, and millions of abortion deaths.

Abortion Among Minorities

One pastoral associate of mine here in Boston, a well-respected black minister, upon learning about the pregnancy health centers opening in Boston, said, "Well, abortion is not a problem in our church. Our people don't have abortions." This is woeful ignorance and wishful thinking. But according to one study, "Abortion Attitudes in the African American Community," this is a strongly believed myth in the black community. According to the study:

> Abortion is viewed by many African Americans as a "white problem"—particularly among men. There appears to be a strong perception that white women are far more likely to have abortions than are African American women. We frequently heard men say, "Our women do not have abortions." While recognizing that abortions occur somewhat more frequently [than the rate expected by men], women also seemed to believe that it was a choice of last resort.[12]

When informed about the actual abortion statistics, many African Americans are appalled. Black women make up only 14 percent of women of childbearing age, but they account for 31.1 percent of all abortions. Hispanic women constitute only 10.6 percent of this same group but suffer 20.2 percent of the total abortions in America. Together, these two minority groups account for less than 25 percent of women of childbearing age in America but account for 51 percent of the total babies aborted in the country.[13] In other words, minority women are aborting at more than twice the rate of white women.

Adding to this tragedy, in public surveys of abortion, minority women poll as more "pro-life" than white women. While 19 percent of the population opposes abortion under any circumstances, 27 percent of all African Americans hold this "no exceptions, no compromise" belief. Only 3 percent endorsed the following position: *Abortion is permissible for any reason the woman chooses at any time during pregnancy; there should be no legal restrictions of any kind; and the government should pay for the procedure if a woman cannot afford the expense.*[14] Such support for unrestricted abortion on demand is currently championed by abortion rights leaders like Senator Hillary Clinton, Planned Parenthood, NARAL (currently calling itself the National Abortion Rights and Reproductive Rights Action League), and the National Organization of Women. Given minority women's heightened sensitivity to the miracle and sanctity of human life, I fear that, for them, the spiritual and emotional devastation from abortion will prove greater as well.

Today almost every third baby conceived in America is killed by abortion.[15] For minority populations, especially, this is tantamount to genocide.

FOUR

The Foundation for Cherishing and Defending Innocent Human Life

In all things, God is preeminent. We love because He loved us first. He calls us to be holy because He is holy. He loves justice and wants us ready to see justice done. In the same way, our passionate commitment to cherish and defend innocent human life is foremost because *God cherishes and defends innocent human life.*

God Is Life

God is Life, and in giving us Himself, He gives us life itself. Or as George Grant writes, "Life is God's gift to the world."[1]

God is the Giver of Life (Acts 17:25), the Fountain of Life (Psalm 36:9), the Defender of Life (Psalm 27:1), the Author of Life (Acts 3:15), and the Restorer of Life (Ruth 4:15).

In sending Jesus Christ into the world, God brings us the Message of Life (Acts 5:20), the Words of Life (John 6:68), the Light of Life (John 8:12), the Gift of New Life (John 5:21), Abundant Life (John 10:10), and Everlasting Life (John 3:16).

To love God is to love life. To be Christlike is to be pro-life. "The pro-life movement and the Christian faith are synonymous. Where there is one, there will be the other—for one cannot be had without the other."[2]

Creation Is Teeming with Life

The life of God has been poured out into all creation. When God created man, his first assignment was to grasp the implications of who God is by studying and naming what he saw all around him (Genesis 2:20). All the natural sciences begin here. The culminating conclusion of naming livestock, the birds of the air, the beasts of the field, and the fish in the seas is that God's world is literally *teeming* with life (Genesis 1:20). This teeming life, with all its phyla and species and families, testifies to the majesty, the radiant beauty, the fierce wrath, the sublime wisdom, and other resplendent qualities of the Giver of life.

Among All that God Has Created, He Especially Cherishes Human Life

When the matter of paying taxes came up, Jesus told the Pharisees to look on the coin and tell Him whose image was on the coin. "Caesar's," they replied. Then Jesus said, "Give to Caesar what is Caesar's, and give to God what is God's" (see Matthew 22:15-22). In saying this, Jesus pointed to what God cherishes above all of creation and endows with a special possessive love. What is it that has God's image stamped onto it and, by this imprint, should be rendered unto God alone? The answer, of course, is human life.

We assert that all human life is sacred and belongs to God because all people are made in the image of God (Genesis 1:27). Since every human being is created by God and in His image, every human being has *intrinsic* rather than *relative* value. People are not valued according to their quality of life or their usefulness to serve the desires of others. They are not to be destroyed when "unwanted." God made them. God wants them and He cherishes them! They are not to be discarded, sacrificed, or euthanized because they are useless to others.

The moral offense of abortion begins here. Like all other forms of homicide, it is an act that defaces the glory of God reflected in the life God is shaping for *His own glory*. Abortion destroys God's property, something He made for His own good purposes.

Among All Human Life, God Especially Cherishes Innocent Human Life

Because God is just and because God values justice, He cherishes *innocent* human life. He therefore calls repeatedly for us to respect and defend the innocent. "Do not put an innocent or honest person to death, for I will not acquit the guilty" (Exodus 23:7). "When men have a dispute, they are to take it to court and the judges will decide the case, acquitting the innocent and condemning the guilty" (Deuteronomy 25:1). "It is not good to punish an innocent man" (Proverbs 17:26). "It is not good to be partial to the wicked or to deprive the innocent of justice" (Proverbs 18:5). "Woe to those who...deny justice to the innocent" (Isaiah 5:22-23).

Among All Forms of Innocent Human Life, God Especially Cherishes Children

This quality is one that we, under normal circumstances, understand quite well. In Boston, while I was writing this section, a three-year-old boy was shot to death while his father was fending off a home invader. The city was shocked. A child! Only three years old! Our outrage and grief is magnified by the fact that it was an innocent *child*. Yes, it is the height of evil to take *any* innocent life. God's justice declares to those who do, "You have fattened yourselves in the day of slaughter. You have condemned and murdered innocent men, who were not opposing you" (James 5:5-6). But judicial sentiment rightly senses the increased moral offense of killing an innocent *child*.

One of Christ's sharpest warnings came when He considered how people injured innocent children by causing them to sin. "If anyone causes one of these little ones who believe in me to sin, it would be better for him to have a large millstone hung around his neck and to be drowned in the depths of the sea" (Matthew 18:6). Since we know that God is just and that His punishment always fits the crime, we can be sure that this fierce punishment is a clear measure of His intense love for the health and well-being of each and every innocent child.

Among All the Innocent Children, God Sees the Preborn Child as His Unique Work of Fashioning Personhood

What can we say about the fetus itself? What does the Bible say about life in the womb? Psalm 139:13-14 says, "You created my inmost being; you knit me together in my mother's womb. I praise you because I am fearfully and wonderfully made."

In this verse, David considers his preborn life in his mother's womb. He sees a "me" in there being made personally by a "you." He sees his life as "God at work." David sees his gestational period not as something impersonal, not a mechanical manufacturing process in which life or personhood is added later like gasoline to a lawnmower to make it run. David sees his mother's womb as God's personal art studio. Gestation is God's unique work of knitting and fashioning and shaping together his "inmost being."

When you look elsewhere in the Bible, you see the same thing. Our lives as persons begin in the womb.

One example is found in Genesis 4:1: "Now Adam knew Eve his wife, and she conceived and bore Cain (NKJV)." In the view of Scripture, it was the *person*, Cain, who was conceived and the *person*, Cain, who was born. Dr. John Davis, professor of theology at Gordon-Conwell Theological Seminary, observes, "The writer's interest in Cain extends back beyond his birth, to his conception. That is when his personal history begins."[3] From the moment of conception the humanity and personhood—the *life*—of Cain began.

The same is true of Job's life. He also saw his personal history as beginning at conception. He said, "Let the day perish on which I was to be born, and the night which said, 'A boy is conceived'" (Job 3:3, NASB). What was conceived? Not a potential boy, something abstract or short of personhood, but a *boy* was conceived.

In the worldview of the Bible, children are children whether inside a womb or inside a house. Genesis 25:22 says of Rebekah, "The children struggled together within her" (NASB). This word for children is the same Hebrew word used for children outside the womb throughout the Old Testament.

Clifford Bajema is correct when he writes in his book *Abortion and the Meaning of Personhood*, "Scripture does not make the kind of subtle philosophical distinctions people make so often today between human life and human being, man and person, life and Life. Scripture just talks about man."[4]

In the New Testament we read that in response to the miraculous conception announced by the angel Gabriel, "Mary got ready and hurried to a town...where she entered Zechariah's home and greeted Elizabeth" (Luke 1:39-40). Just days after conceiving, Mary met Elizabeth, who was at that time six months pregnant with her preborn child, John the Baptist. Luke 1:41-44 says, "When Elizabeth heard Mary's greeting, the baby leaped in her womb and...in a loud voice [Elizabeth] exclaimed: '...as soon as the sound of your greeting reached my ears, the baby in my womb leaped for joy.'"

This word *baby* (the Greek word *brephos*) is the same word used in Luke 2:12 and 2:16 for the baby Jesus as a newborn child: "You will find a baby wrapped in cloths and lying in a manger" (v. 12).

In addition, Elizabeth's encounter with Mary stresses, with a sense of wondrous surprise to Elizabeth, the personhood of both the preborn John the Baptist and the Christ child. Elizabeth feels her own baby's reaction at being in the presence of the promised Messiah. The preborn baby, John the Baptist, leaped with joy at the presence of the preborn person who was Jesus Christ the Almighty!

Now consider how far along Christ was at this moment in terms of His embryonic development. The phrase "at that time" in Luke 1:39 indicates that immediately after the announced conception, Mary set off to visit Elizabeth. Our text says she "hurried" to see her. Since the distance was at most only a few days' travel away, Jesus was a mere zygote, conceived just days before. Yet, wondrously, when Mary greeted Elizabeth, the six-month-old fetus, John the Baptist, felt *joy* in the presence of the incarnate, fully human, Son of God.

FIVE

Healing for the Morally Blind

Most of the time we take for granted that everyone knows what a human being is. I have never heard a mother give birth and wonder, "But is my baby a real human being yet?" Humanity and personhood are self-evident. Legal abortion, like legal slavery in the past, requires us to deny what is self-evident. One can see it plainly by the natural sciences and by natural law, if self-interest does not get in the way.

Human Embryology

Dr. Hymie Gordon of the Mayo Clinic said, "By all the criteria of modern molecular biology, life is present from the moment of conception."[1] Every single biology textbook in the world agrees with Dr. Gordon. At conception all of the genetic material that we shall ever have, at all stages of human development (zygote, embryo, fetus, newborn, infant, toddler, child, adolescent, teenager, adult, senior, and so on) is present. Preborn children are not *becoming* human; they are as John Stott said, growing "into the fullness of humanity that they already possess."[2]

The wonderful science of embryology, together with advances in technology, especially ultrasound, have allowed us to see, photograph, and film in living color what King David so poetically meditated upon in Psalm 139:13-14. "You knit me together in my mother's womb. I praise you because I am fearfully and wonderfully made."

A fertilized human egg becomes a self-directed entity when it multiplies into only four cells. The baby's heart starts beating as early as the 18th day (about 31 days from the first day of a woman's last menstrual period), just as a woman misses her period and wonders if she is pregnant.[3] Surgical abortions are usually not performed before seven weeks (49 days from the first day of a woman's last menstrual period).[4] By that time, the baby has identifiable arms and legs (day 45) and has measurable brain waves (about 40 days). During the seventh through the 10th weeks, when 61 percent of all abortions are performed, fingers and genitals appear and the child's face is recognizably human. At six weeks all the major organs are formed, and by 12 weeks no new anatomical developments occur. The baby is only growing bigger.

Yet in this country there are 400 abortions performed *every day* on babies in their second and third trimesters. They are not done to save the life of the mother. They are done for the same reasons earlier abortions are done. The right to abortion, as it stands now, allows a woman to abort her baby at any time for any reason or no reason.[5]

Ultrasound and the Empirical Observations of Dr. Bernard Nathanson

From a biblical standpoint, as already shown, there is no difference between being a human being and being a person. The difference does not exist empirically either.

Dr. Bernard Nathanson was responsible for

75,000 abortions in New York in the late 1960s and early 1970s. He was one of the main architects of strategies designed to legalize abortion in America. It was ultrasound, invented in the 1970s, that became for him a window to the womb. He said:

> From then on we could see this person in the womb from the very beginning—and study and measure it and weigh it and take care of it and treat it and diagnose it and do all kinds of things. It became, in essence, a second patient. Now a patient is a person. So basically I was dealing then with two people, instead of just one carrying some lump of meat around. That's what started me doubting the ethical acceptability of abortion on request.[6]

Dr. Nathanson's acknowledgement of the personhood of the preborn child had no conscious religious tone to it. Dr. Nathanson was an atheistic Jew. "I had not a seedling of faith to nourish me," he wrote.[7] Embryology itself, confirmed by ultrasound, led him to acknowledge the personhood of preborn children.

The *New England Journal of Medicine* reported back in 1983 that ultrasound was teaching us to see the preborn child as a "patient."

> Ultrasound imagery will probably change the way in which we view the fetus with a diagnosed and treatable disorder…Indeed, surgeons already regard the fetus with a correctable congenital defect as a "patient."[8]

The same report also indicated that ultrasound examinations were turning ambivalent mothers toward parenthood and away from abortion.

> One of us pointed to the small, visibly moving fetal form on the screen and asked, "How do you feel about seeing what is inside you?" She answered crisply, "It certainly makes you think twice about abortion!…I feel that it is human. It belongs to me. I could never have an abortion now."

The Question of "Full" Personhood

Is there a difference between being human and being a person? Abortion advocates justify abortion (and infanticide and euthanasia) by making a distinction between being human and being a person. They propose that the right to life is limited to those who are "full" persons rather than merely human.

For example, Peter Singer, in a famous debate held at Princeton, advocated expanding abortion rights to infanticide. "I do not think it is always wrong to kill an innocent human being. Simply killing an infant is never equivalent to killing a person."[9]

We have already shown that according to the Bible, no such distinction exists. Even more, ask yourself, "Is it even reasonable?" One way to see the fallacy that one can be human but not be a person is to ask, "What is the difference? What characterizes a human being who is not a person?"

The most common argument has to do with consciousness. It is argued that one is a person only if one is "fully" conscious, whatever that is. Proponents of this position cannot define consciousness. Nor will they apply the principle across the board. Different levels of consciousness and awareness can be seen between any two people. A 50-year-old is more "aware," in general, than a teenager. Does this justify killing teenagers because, while human, they are not yet "full" persons? Of course not. Besides, they would fight back. There might even be different levels of self-awareness between two ethics professors. But Singer would not agree that simply killing an ethics professor is never equivalent to killing a person. He would defend his right to life loudly. No, Singer-type ethicists always pick defenseless groups (babies, the infirm, the mentally ill, or disenfranchised racial groups). Such people cannot defend themselves.

But they can appeal to God, "Let your compassion come to me that I may live" (Psalm 119:77). And the God who made them and cherishes them hears their cry for justice and sends His people into the breach, commanding them, "Speak up for those who cannot speak for themselves" (Proverbs 31:8) and "Defend the rights of the poor and needy" (31:9). If we do not come to their defense, they have no hope.

Another answer offered to justify making a distinction between being human and being a person is size. We look at a six-week-old preborn child and say it is too small to be a full person. But do we really believe that the bigger a person is, the more rights he has? Men are generally larger than women; older siblings are usually bigger than the younger ones. But in neither case do we say that the larger person is superior to the smaller.

We look at a five-week-old preborn child and it looks odd to us. All the more for a five-day-old baby in the womb. We conclude that it cannot be a person because it looks different from what we usually see and are familiar with. But think for a minute. Newborns are odd-looking too. They have oversized heads, way out of proportion to the rest of their bodies. It is only because we have seen so many of them at this stage that we are used to it. Size, shape, and proportion do not determine personhood. They reflect the variety and wonder of human life at different stages.

Still another claim is "viability." But like the unborn child, a newborn cannot survive without help either. If I find a two-year-old lost in the city on a snowy night, he will most likely die without my help. Do I say, "He is nonviable. He won't make it out here by himself. I think I will kill him"? Is that acceptable? No. Although he depends on me to stay alive, he is a precious child and worthy of my aid. People of any age, dependent on a heart machine during surgery or a breathing machine afterward, are not "viable" per se (able to live on their own). But do they cease to be persons? Of course not.

The Eclipse of Reason

Bernard Nathanson rightly notes that the applied language of "personhood" has always been exclusive in history. During the Holocaust, Jews (as well as Gypsies and Poles and Roman Catholic priests) were widely classified as nonpersons. Likewise, blacks in America suffered the same treatment under the infamous Dred Scott ruling that upheld the practice of slavery.

Corrupt language, and you corrupt thought. Abortion is like that. It demands normalizing the abnormal. It requires redefinition and schizophrenic reasoning, or as Nathanson calls it, "The eclipse of reason."

If a drunk driver kills a mother on her way to the hospital for a prenatal checkup, the killer can be charged with a *double* homicide. Yet if she makes it safely to the hospital but changes her mind about having another child, she can have the baby removed piece by piece or delivered breech in the ghastly infanticide procedure misnamed the "partial birth" abortion.

In Massachusetts, a pregnant mother was put in jail because the Department of Social Services feared she might hurt her *preborn* baby. She belonged to a small religious sect that did not believe in using modern medicine and hospitals in caring for their children. The State argued that they had a compelling interest to protect the health of the preborn baby and make sure the baby got medical help upon delivery if need be. Yet if this mother declared her "reproductive rights" and insisted on an abortion, they would have taken her to an abortion facility. In Massachusetts, the State would even have had to pay for it.

In the summer of 2000, a flurry of e-mail arrived telling me about an astounding picture of a human hand. In the photo, a 21-week-old preborn, Samuel Alexander Armes, reaches out from his mother's womb to clasp the finger of the surgeon who is about to save his life. Baby Samuel, undergoing surgery for spina bifida, had yet to take his first breath, yet his grip, so sure and firm, spoke loudly. "I am here. I am alive. I am counting on you. I am grateful."

For a moment, the nation understood what Sir Charles Bell, one of the most respected comparative anatomists of the nineteenth century, once declared: "No serious account of human life can ignore the importance of the human hand."[10]

"The human hand is so beautifully formed," observed Bell, "its actions are so powerful, so free and yet so delicate, that there is no thought of its complexity as an instrument; we use it as we draw our breath, unconsciously."

Bell was providing an early rebuttal to Darwin's theory of evolution at the time. Divine proportion was at work. In the human hand, the Perfect Craftsman wrote His signature.

Little baby Samuel's hand gripping the surgeon's glove woke the conscience of a nation, be it ever so briefly, that the preborn is *self-evidently* a human being. Look at the picture! Abortion is *self-evidently* the violent destruction of a human being. This truth I have carried with me for some years, strangely, in the form of a human hand. In 1989, a friend of mine pulled a tiny hand from the rubbish behind my local abortion facility. If the first picture is a wonder, the second is a crime against humanity. If baby Samuel's little grip says, "Thank you!" what does this unnamed baby's hand say but, "I am here too. Won't someone save my life? Why are they hurting me?"

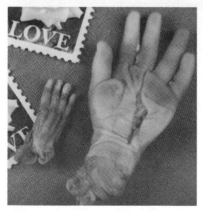

Photo: Michael Clancy. Used by permission.

Six

The Greatest Moral Evil of Our Time

Dr. James Dobson said, "I consider abortion to be the greatest moral evil of our time, because of the worth of those little babies." Is Dobson correct? Does abortion rise to that level, or is it just one social evil among equals (homelessness, fatherlessness, hunger, etc.)?

There is a tendency to reduce abortion to an "issue." I find it hard to write about abortion without using the word. Certainly there are many legitimate issues vying for our attention. But abortion is an act of violence that kills a baby. As such, it goes beyond our senses, beyond our vocabulary, beyond the boundaries of normal discourse. It shares the same mind-numbing, too-horrifying-to-be-true quality that the specter of the Holocaust raised for the previous generation. The numbers are now so large and the implications of our guilt so great that we experience something of an intellectual coma from the trauma of it. We simply shut down. We do this by reducing abortion to one issue among many and then choosing other issues to focus on. But I think Dobson is correct. Abortion is the greatest moral evil of our age. It is the social injustice that most inflames the heart of God and for which we, His people, are called to act with profound and persistent moral courage. I offer the following reasons for this conclusion.

Among All the Offenses of Man, the Greatest Offense Is Shedding Innocent Human Blood

God is long-suffering. But there is a limit to His patience. There is a point when, through the hardness of our hearts, we become so callous to the moral will of God that He says, "Enough!" In Noah's time, the maturation of evil reached that point. "Then the LORD said, 'My Spirit will not contend with man forever'" (Genesis 6:3). Then He "wiped" the earth clean in righteous judgment (6:7).

In tracing out the breaking point when God moves from patiently warning to active judgment, Scripture says it is the killing of innocent people, or passively accepting the killing of innocent people, that finally invokes His wrath.

This is the message of the prophets. Some prophets brought this message as an indictment. Others brought it as a reminder as to why judgment fell. In both cases, they pointed to the shedding of innocent blood as the point when God's patience reached its end and God said, "Enough!" Consider the prophet Ezekiel:

> This is what the Sovereign LORD says: O city that brings on herself doom by shedding blood in her midst…you have become guilty because of the blood you have shed. (Ezekiel 22:3-4)

Isaiah also indicted the people for their bloodguilt.

When you spread out your hands in prayer,
I will hide my eyes from you; even if you
offer many prayers, I will not listen. Your
hands are full of blood; wash and make
yourselves clean. (Isaiah 1:15-16)

In Revelation 16:5-6, God's judgment is
described as vindication for those whose blood
was shed unjustly. God is personally and inti-
mately watching over each person's life, even during martyrdom. "You are just in these
judgments...for they have shed the blood of your
saints and prophets." In Genesis 4:10, we catch a
glimpse of how God cares for innocent human
life. When Cain killed his brother Abel, God
heard Abel cry out for vindication. "Listen! Your
brother's blood cries out to me from the ground."

Because God loves, He gets angry. Because He
cherishes innocent human life with a burning
heart and commands all men everywhere to do
the same, His revulsion at the murder of the innocents knows no limit, nor does His wrath when it
is finally unleashed. God's wrath is called "fierce"
(1 Samuel 28:18), "furious" (Job 40:11), "full"
(Psalm 78:38), "consuming" (Psalm 59:13),

"great" (Psalm 102:10), and "jealous" (Ezekiel 36:6). For God to warn us of His wrath is another sign of His love. For us to ignore it is a sign of how hardened we have become and how ripe we are to receive His wrath.

Among All the Ways Men Shed Innocent Blood, the Most Offensive is Child Sacrifice

There are many ways to shed innocent blood, but the most heinous form is child sacrifice. In child sacrifice, that which God cherishes is destroyed in order to worship false gods. One cannot profane the glory of God by any greater means. So Israel was taught, "Do not give any of your children to be sacrificed to Molech, for you must not profane the name of your God. I am the LORD" (Leviticus 18:21).

In God's eyes, both child sacrifice and the passive acceptance of child sacrifice profane God's name and arouse His indignation. So He taught the people of Israel,

> Any Israelite or any alien living in Israel who gives any of his children to Molech must be put to death....I will set my face

against that man and I will cut him off
from his people; for by giving his children
to Molech, he has defiled my sanctuary and
profaned my holy name. If the people of
the community close their eyes when that
man gives one of his children to Molech
and they fail to put him to death, I will set
my face against that man and his family
and will cut off from their people both him
and all who follow him in prostituting
themselves to Molech. (Leviticus 20:2-5)

Israel was to have no part in the shedding of
innocent blood of children. They were to avoid it
and oppose it as the very antithesis of what pleases
the true and living God. He warned Israel that if
they followed the same practices of the people He
was wiping off the land, they too would be wiped
away (for God treats all men equally before His
holy law). When God wanted to emphasize what
sort of practices were to be avoided, and what it
was particularly that so offended Him and
invoked His unrestrained wrath, what did He
point to? He pointed again to the shedding of
innocent blood of children.

You must not worship the LORD your God
in their way, because in worshiping their
gods, they do all kinds of detestable things
the LORD hates. They even burn their sons
and daughters in the fire as sacrifices to
their gods. (Deuteronomy 12:31)

God's patience with sinful man reaches its end
when innocent children are sacrificed.

In spite of these warnings, Israel later on fell
so far away from the heart of God that they did
imitate the sins of the Canaanites.

Ahaz, king of Judah, "did not do what was
right in the eyes of the LORD his God. He walked
in the ways of the kings of Israel and even sacrificed
his son in the fire, following the detestable ways of
the nations the LORD had driven out before the
Israelites" (2 Kings 16:2-3). Ahaz comes to represent the pinnacle of moral corruption in Israel
because he reached the pinnacle of moral offense:
He terminated the life of his own child.

Israel and Judah both suffered exile in due
course. The kingdom of Israel was wiped out first.
"The king of Assyria invaded the entire land...
[and] captured Samaria and deported the Israelites

to Assyria" (2 Kings 17:5-6). The people were not left to wonder why. "All this took place because the Israelites had sinned against the LORD their God" (17:7). What follows is a formal indictment of all their offenses. The last on the list, the final expression of divine disgust, is this: "They sacrificed their sons and daughters in the fire. They practiced divination and sorcery and sold themselves to do evil in the eyes of the LORD, provoking him to anger" (17:17).

Perhaps the clearest expression of God's outrage against the slaughter of innocent children is found in Ezekiel 16:20-21. Here child sacrifice is recorded in very personal terms. "And you took your sons and daughters whom you bore to me and sacrificed them as food to the idols. Was your prostitution not enough? You slaughtered my children and sacrificed them to the idols."

God takes the death of every child personally; He takes the slaughter of innocent children as nothing less than the murder of His own children.

Abortion Is Child Sacrifice

Whatever the reasons we cling to in order to justify abortion, they are no match for what the conscience knows and Scripture confirms is "child sacrifice." We want our lives to go according to our plans. The baby is sacrificed to secure them. Kim Flodin, a staunch defender of abortion rights and a freelance writer, had two abortions. She wrote of her anguishing circumstances and subsequent guilt and injuries for *Newsweek* magazine. She concluded, "I was pregnant, I carried two unborn children and I chose, for completely selfish reasons, to deny them life so that I could better my own."[1] This is child sacrifice.

We no longer sacrifice our children to please some pagan, bloodthirsty god like Molech. We have made ourselves into a god and sacrifice our children for our own ends. We abort because of money, believing we cannot afford a child *and* do the other things we want to do with our money. We abort to save ourselves the embarrassment of others discovering our promiscuity and to save our reputations. We abort to save relationships or educational and vocational goals we have planned. There are many understandable reasons for abortion. But they are all penultimate reasons. The ultimate reason we abort is selfishness and a lack of faith in God. Or as James 4:2 says, "You want something but don't get it. You kill and covet, but you cannot have what you want." Not everyone comes to see it as honestly as Kim Flodin does, but that in a nutshell is what abortion is all about. Abortion is killing so that we may get something else. As such, abortion is a substitute for prayer. "You do not have, because you do not ask God."

In this sense, abortion serves as the deadly "apple" enticing every Adam and Eve to cast away humble, glad dependence on God's provision as our Creator. It calls into question the wisdom and goodness of God Himself and His creative prerogatives. It promises us the power to define our own lives. It defies His will and declares, "My will be done!" Bloodguilt and death at every level of our being flow from it.

SEVEN

Cherishing and Defending Innocent Human Life

How, then, shall we live? What must we do if we are to hold each life precious? If we are to cherish and defend innocent human life, what divine precepts must be reaffirmed? I think of three.

First, We Are Not to Shed Innocent Blood Ourselves

This law has been written on every human heart, in every culture, in every age. "The sacredness of life gives rise to its inviolability, written from the beginning in man's heart, in his conscience. The question: 'What have you done?' (Genesis 4:10), which God addresses to Cain after he has killed his brother Abel, interprets the experience of every person; in the depths of his conscience, man is always reminded of the inviolability of life—his own life and that of others—as something which does not belong to him, because it is the property and gift of God the Creator and Father."[1]

What rings true as natural law is amplified in the Ten Commandments. Exodus 20:13 says simply, "You shall not murder." The civil laws of justice and mercy, when given to Israel, included, "Have nothing to do with a false charge and do not put an innocent or honest person to death, for I will not acquit the guilty" (Exodus 23:7).

Human life, being God's chief delight in His creation, is protected by these moral absolutes. In opposing abortion, we are not imposing a morality distinctive to Christianity. We are defending the common justice due to all people of every race and of every faith (or no faith). Every human being innately desires his life to be respected. The right to life is the foundation for both civil justice and peace, making way for the freedom to choose what we perceive promises us the most happiness.

Virginia Ramey Mollenkott, professor emeritus at William Paterson University in New Jersey, calls herself an "evangelical feminist." She claims that "nowhere does the Bible prohibit abortion."[2] In one sense she is right. The word abortion does not appear in the Bible. Of course, the Bible does not prohibit "driving to endanger" or "domestic violence" or "killing five-year-olds" either, if you demand an explicit listing for something to be forbidden. The Bible teaches that abortion is wrong by teaching us that God views the preborn child as a person, and then by calling us to protect the life of all people from homicide.

What about people conceived by rape or incest? Isn't abortion an appropriate remedy in such cases? You have to be cruel beyond measure not to ache for victims of such violence and yearn to help in some way. But it is foolish to believe that killing what at that moment God is personally knitting together with great joy could ever be helpful. The right to life and the prohibition against killing stand as moral absolutes against the ever-swirling tides of emotions and misguided sympathies that create "exceptions" that justify killing the innocent. We delude only ourselves to argue that it is wrong to destroy a preborn baby "except in cases of rape or incest."[3] The external circumstance under which a child is conceived does not cancel that child's inherent worth.

God is as much the true Creator and Sovereign Lord of Ethel Waters as He is of a child conceived in love. Ethel, the famous gospel singer who worked with Billy Graham for so many years, was conceived when her 12-year-old mother was raped.[4] *All* human life is valued and worthy of our defense, because everyone, without exception, is created in God's image. God is sovereign and works His good and perfect will through even the most painful events that may come our way. To make exceptions is to deny the sanctity of life ethic and follow the quality of life ethic that fuels abortion in the first place.

The divine command "You shall not murder" prohibits us from killing human beings to relieve pain or poverty or perceived suffering of any kind. We do not love the infirm or the deformed or the handicapped by *killing* them. Love does not kill; it shares in the burden that pain and suffering causes. That is the very definition of compassion: "to suffer with." The response of God's people to the problems of poverty and need is to answer affirmatively to Isaiah 58:6-7:

> Is not this the kind of fasting I have chosen: to loose the chains of injustice and untie the cords of the yoke, to set the oppressed free and break every yoke? Is it not to share your food with the hungry and to provide the poor wanderer with shelter—when you see the naked, to clothe him, and not to turn away from your own flesh and blood?

There is never a justifiable reason to shed the blood of an innocent human being.[5]

Second, We Are Not to Accept the Shedding of Innocent Blood by Others

In Deuteronomy 21:1-9, Israel is instructed how to respond to the murder of an innocent man in its midst. The distance to the body was to be measured to determine jurisdiction. The closest town was to take responsibility for it. Normal life was suspended. With great solemnity, the spiritual leaders, the priests and Levites, along with the judicial leaders, would lead the people through elaborate and costly rituals to ensure that God's revulsion at the shedding of innocent blood was a matter deeply imprinted on the hearts and minds of the people.

> Then the elders of the town nearest the body shall take a heifer that has never been worked and has never worn a yoke and lead her down to a valley that has not been plowed or planted and where there is a flowing stream. There in the valley they are to break the heifer's neck. (21:3-4)

For those of us in leadership roles in the church this passage ought to be especially instructive. The death of the innocent requires moral interpretation by its leaders, or people will accommodate themselves to it. Leaders must lead! The profound lesson they are to impress upon the people is that the death of the innocent diminishes everyone. By taking people out of their routine and by bringing forth a perfectly good heifer and sacrificing it on prime commercial real estate, making it holy (unusable) space, Israel would feel in the loss of her precious time and property what

God values for eternity: human life. Likewise, these ceremonies would reaffirm the social contract to be our brother's keeper. They would provide an avenue for the community to reaffirm the value of human life.

Whenever the innocent are killed, no matter who they are, known or unknown, big or small, the Deuteronomic law instructs the spiritual leaders of the community to rearticulate the pro-life ethic. The people are to *hear* that the taking of innocent life or the passive acceptance of the death of the innocent is horrifyingly unacceptable.

God directs the spiritual leaders of the community to clearly and solemnly instruct the people regarding the shedding of innocent blood:

> The priests, the sons of Levi, shall step forward…and they shall declare: "Our hands did not shed this blood, nor did our eyes see it done. Accept this atonement for your people Israel, whom you have redeemed, O LORD, and do not hold your people guilty of the blood of an innocent man." And the bloodshed will be atoned for. So you will purge from yourselves the guilt of shedding

innocent blood, since you have done what
is right in the eyes of the LORD. (Deuteronomy 21:5, 7-9)

Notice that even though the community itself
was not guilty of shedding innocent blood and
could honestly say, "We did not do it, nor see it
done," Israel would still share in the judgment of
God *if the leaders did not lead the people to openly
and jointly renounce the shedding of innocent blood.*
By leading the people through this costly process
of resensitizing their hearts to the preciousness of
human life, Israel's spiritual leaders purged real
guilt that otherwise would have been theirs corporately to answer for.

That's because passive acceptance of murder
would immediately coarsen the heart of everyone.
And hard-heartedness is itself sinful. By praying
and sacrificing the heifer (a precursor to the purg-
ing of guilt that the sacrifice of Christ would
bring), Israel's leaders would ensure the opposite
effect: that God's people would cherish innocent
life.

This is the right thing to do. Or as verse 9 says
to both the leaders and the people as a whole,

"You have done what is right in the eyes of the LORD." I take this to mean that for God's people, it is right and necessary at times to openly and corporately grieve and recommit our lives to holding each life precious. And it means that it is right and necessary for leaders to lead God's people through this grieving and recommitment process. And it is wrong if we do not.

With reference to abortion today, we are facing the death of the innocent and it is diminishing us all; we just don't sense or feel it. If we, as spiritual leaders, do not grab our people and lead them to grieve and mourn the loss, then together our hardened hearts will grow even harder. The peace that we feel will not be peace; it will be deadness. After all, an entire book of the Bible is set aside for corporate *lamentation*.

We, too, must set aside some time to focus on what the loss of life means. We must challenge people to make financial sacrifices to those efforts that reassert the value of life in the popular culture. We must do it not only so that such ministries can flourish; we must also do it for our own sakes—that our hearts will not grow coarsened along with the popular culture. When Jesus said,

"Where your treasure is, there your heart will be also" (Matthew 6:21), it is our hearts that He had in view.

In addition to corporately grieving the bloodshed of abortion and publicly acknowledging the damage and guilt it has wrought to us all, every community of faith can set aside and dedicate certain spaces to the reaffirmation of our commitment to cherish and defend innocent human life. The Israelites were instructed to set aside some real estate—"a valley with a flowing spring"—for this very purpose. Crisis pregnancy centers are often places taken out of commercial use by the Christian community and dedicated to providing life-affirming assistance to women and couples in pregnancy distress. This proactive effort is in keeping with God's command that we actually *rescue* the innocent.

Third, We Are to Defend the Weak and Rescue the Innocent

In Luke 10:37, Jesus illustrates authentic love by pointing to the personal intervention of the Good Samaritan and commanding, "Go and do likewise."

This is the law of love. It flows *from* love for God and *to* one's neighbors. Indeed, so absolute is the source and course of God's love that love for a neighbor is the proving ground for love for God. "If anyone...sees his brother in need but has no pity on him, how can the love of God be in him?" (1 John 3:17). It is not possible. To illustrate, Jesus told this parable:

A man was going down from Jerusalem to Jericho, when he fell into the hands of robbers. They stripped him of his clothes, beat him and went away, leaving him half dead. A priest happened to be going down the same road, and when he saw the man, he passed by on the other side. So too, a Levite, when he came to the place and saw him, passed by on the other side. But a Samaritan, as he traveled, came where the man was; and when he saw him, he took pity on him, He went to him and bandaged his wounds, pouring on oil and wine. Then he put the man on his own donkey, took him to an inn and took care of him. The next day he took out two silver coins and gave them to the innkeeper. "Look after him," he said, "and when I return, I will reimburse you for any extra expense you may have." (Luke 10:30-35)

Love is a powerful force in the human heart. Love sees people as neighbors or brothers, not strangers or nonpersons. Love makes us willing to look at the plight of others, when self-interest prefers ignorance. Love draws us near to the crisis. Without love, we steer clear. Love grieves and weeps. It is moved with compassion and pity, but love is not satisfied with remorse alone.

The priest and the Levite might have muttered, as they hurried on to their Bible study or prayer meeting or whatever was on their schedule, "How sad, how terrible. The world is going to hell in a handbasket." But genuine love does not only sorrow over death, it moves toward death—not away from it. Love rushes into the breach like white corpuscles rush to a wound. Love made the Samaritan stop and *draw* near. Love *picked* the man up, *bandaged* his wounds, *put* him on a donkey, and *took* him to an inn. When the innkeeper asked, "And to whom shall I address the bill?" love responded, "Well, until I can find out who this brother is and what resources he has, send the bill to me." Love *paid* the bill. This is Christianity in verbs.

For this reason, it is not enough to say, "I did not have an abortion," any more than the demands of love would have been met if the Samaritan had said, "Well, I did not beat this man." Love demands more and love empowers more.

It demands personal involvement at the expense of predetermined plans and schedules. Love asks, "What does the law of love require of me in this situation?" Then those who love God do it to the best of their ability.

In commanding us to "go and do likewise" (Matthew 10:37), Jesus could just as easily have quoted Scripture. He could have pointed to Psalm 82:3-4:

> Defend the cause of the weak and father-
> less; maintain the rights of the poor and
> oppressed. Rescue the weak and needy;
> deliver them from the hand of the wicked.

He could have quoted Proverbs 31:8-9,

Speak up for those who cannot speak for
themselves, for the rights of all who are des-
titute. Speak up and judge fairly; defend
the rights of the poor and needy.

Courage Required and Supplied

Love is so powerful that love will speak up for
those who have no voice. Love will defend those
who are being pressured and coerced by others.
Love will rescue the innocent from those who
would harm them. Of course, none of this could
happen unless love also produces courage. But it
does.

In giving us these commandments, God
acknowledges that there are times when cherishing and defending innocent human life may cost
us dearly. He commands us nonetheless, because
He also promises to supply the faith and courage
needed to carry it out. Proverbs 24:10-12 says:

If you falter in times of trouble, how small
is your strength! Rescue those being led
away to death; hold back those staggering
toward slaughter. If you say, "But we knew
nothing about this," does not he who

weighs the heart perceive it? Does not he
who guards your life know it? Will he not
repay each person according to what he has
done?

These "times of trouble" are serious and trying; innocents are being slaughtered. It might be
state-sanctioned killing or the illegal action of a
wicked individual or mob. No "context" is given
for the command to "rescue those being led away
to death." If a specific context were described, we
might limit application of the command to that
group instead of applying the command whenever
any individual or group is dehumanized and killed
to serve the purposes of others. Difficult and
costly as it may be, in such times we are commanded to actively oppose the slaughter of the
innocent and to rescue them if possible.

In a strange way, we will know precisely when
this passage from Proverbs is to be applied by the
way we convince ourselves that it doesn't apply.
Verse 12 says, "If you say, 'But we knew nothing
about this,' does not he who weighs the heart perceive it?" This verse takes direct aim at cowardice
clothed as ignorance or busyness. When we are

saying to ourselves, *I didn't know, I didn't realize, I had no idea,* it is time to be honest. We are afraid to know the truth.

We all have an intuitive understanding that if we defend an innocent person who is under imminent attack, we shall not be treated any more kindly by his or her oppressor. If I see a man beating a woman and come to her aid, I am likely to get a beating too.

When the state dehumanizes one group of people and sanctions their "termination," speaking up on their behalf is costly; it can be dangerous to one's own life. It does require of us courage. Proverbs 24:12 teaches us that courage is required. It also teaches us that courage is supplied through our *faith in God.*

Verse 12 says, "Does not he who guards your life know it? Will he not repay each person according to what he has done?" I do not take these words to be advocating some meritorious formula for saving grace. Faith in God is saving. And in "times of trouble" one's faith in God is demonstrated by the confidence and trust found in saying, "God is guarding my life." People with this kind of faith in God are free then to aid others—in this case, the weak and the innocent. Failure to do so means that our confession is proven shallow and empty ("If you falter in times of trouble, how small is your strength!"). Therefore, God will judge us faithless by our cowardly actions or faithful by our moral courage. If we put our faith in God, we will have the courage to rescue the innocent.

Martin Luther said,

> If I profess with the loudest voice and the clearest exposition every portion of the truth of God except precisely that point which the world and the devil are at that moment attacking, I am not confessing Christ. Where the battle rages, there the loyalty of the soldier is proven, and to be steady on all the battle-fronts besides is mere flight and disgrace if he flinches at that point.[6]

In this postmodern culture, it is fairly easy to be a Christian, except when it comes to faithfully upholding God's lordship over matters of sexuality and life. We are flinching on that point. Our "time of trouble" comes when we faithfully defend God's right to define and govern our sexuality, and uphold the value of every preborn life. The great test of our faithfulness is whether we will curry the favor of men by holding silent and timid, or we will please God by speaking up for, defending, and rescuing our tiniest of brothers and sisters from the violence of abortion.

Which of These Was the Good Neighbor?

I find that historical examples help greatly in inspiring us to cherish and defend human life. In every age, the attack varies in its target; but ever since Adam and Eve and Cain and Abel, there has been one constant. Death has always been seen as a solution to problems. Before returning to the challenge of the present hour, let us consider some who have faced the great test already.

Eva Fogalman, in her book *Conscience and Courage: Rescuers of Jews During the Holocaust,* gives us a glorious example of what "go and do likewise" means to those committed to following the law of love.

> In 1942, Wladyslaw Misiuna, a teenager
> from Radom, Poland, was recruited by the
> Germans to help inmates at the Fila

Majdanek concentration camp start a
rabbit farm to supply furs for soldiers at the
Russian front. Wladyslaw felt responsible
for the thirty young women he supervised.
He stuffed his coat pockets with bread,
milk, carrots, and pilfered potatoes and
smuggled the food to them. But one day
one of his workers, Devora Salzberg, con-
tracted a mysterious infection. Wladyslaw
was beside himself. He knew if the Germans
discovered the open lesions on her arms
they would kill her. Wladyslaw knew that
to save Devora he needed to cure her. But
how? He took the simplest route. He
infected himself with her blood and went
to a doctor in town. The doctor prescribed
a medication, which Wladyslaw then
shared with Devora. Both were cured, and
both survived the war.[7]

When I ask myself what it is about this story
that glorifies God and satisfies my soul, I think of
several reasons. Misiuna chose good over evil. He
demonstrated a clear commitment to cherish and
defend innocent human life. He showed great

moral courage. He was practical yet creative in his life-saving plan. But over all this, his actions imitate the very gospel of Jesus Christ. For "greater love has no one than this, that he lay down his life for his friends" (John 15:13).

In contrast, consider another story from the same "troubled time." In *The Hiding Place*, Corrie Ten Boom writes of the time when her family had taken in a young Jewish mother and her baby. When the local pastor came calling, Corrie put the great test before him:

> "Would you be willing to take a Jewish mother and her baby into your home? They will almost certainly be arrested otherwise."
>
> Color drained from the man's face. He took a step back from me. "Miss Ten Boom! I do hope you're not involved with any of this illegal concealment and under-cover business. It's just not safe! Think of your father! And your sister—she's never been strong!"
>
> On impulse I told the pastor to wait and ran upstairs....I asked the mother's per-

mission to borrow the infant....Back in the
dining room I pulled back the coverlet
from the baby's face.

There was a long silence. The man
bent forward, his hand in spite of himself
reaching for the tiny fist curled round the
blanket. For a moment I saw compassion
and fear struggle in his face. Then he
straightened. "No. Definitely not. We
could lose our lives for that Jewish child!"

Unseen by either of us, Father had
appeared in the doorway. "Give the child to
me, Corrie," he said.

Father held the baby close, his white
beard brushing its cheek....At last he
looked up at the pastor. "You say we could
lose our lives for this child. I would consider that the greatest honor that could
come to my family."

The pastor turned sharply on his heels
and walked out of the room.[8]

In one account we have a young teenage boy;
in the other a trained and experienced pastor. Now
which of these was the good neighbor? Which

followed the law of love? Which one makes the Christian faith compellingly attractive? Which one is forgettable (along with his faith)? Which one must we follow in our "times of trouble" no matter how unpopular or costly?

Only the sort of Christian community that cherishes and defends innocent human life will ever be able to speak authoritatively and winsomely about the need for a new and transformed life. If we do not love and defend the innocent, we will have no moral authority to speak about God's love for the guilty. The law of love makes them inseparable. And because we love both the innocent and the guilty, and because we live in a culture of death with its ever-hardening hearts of unbelief, we must follow Winston Churchill's advice when declaring the gospel to the guilty and declaring protection for the weak:

> If you have an important point to make, don't try to be subtle or clever. Use a pile driver. Hit the point once. Then come back and hit it again. Then hit it a third time—a tremendous whack.[9]

/ EIGHT /

The History of God's People Cherishing and Defending Innocent Human Life

Throughout history God's people have waged a war of love against all things that destroy body and soul. Beginning with the biblical record, we see a long and glorious record of people who cherished and defended innocent human life.

Reuben rescued Joseph from being killed by his own brothers (Genesis 37:21-22). The Hebrew midwives rescued baby boys from the infanticide of Pharaoh (Exodus 1:17). The soldiers of Saul rescued Jonathan from murder (1 Samuel 14:45). Obadiah rescued 100 prophets from

Jezebel and provided food and shelter for them (1 Kings 18:4). Esther risked her life to save her people from a royal (legalized) call for genocide (Esther 4:14; 7:3-4).

All these godly heroes understood the law of love. They understood the demands that love makes. They did not shrink back in fear of the consequences that obedience to the law of love would bring.

Christianity from its very beginning has waged a fierce and steady battle against the ancient and unrelenting practices of paganism: abortion, infanticide, exposure, and abandonment of innocent babies.

The world into which Christianity was seeded saw nothing wrong with these crimes. In Rome, babies were abandoned outside the city walls to die from exposure or become food for wild beasts. Abortifacient concoctions, using herbs, pessaries, and poisons are well documented in Greek, Persian, Chinese, Arab, and Egyptian cultures. Infanticide was ritualized among Canaanite peoples; they burned babies in pyres as offerings to Molech. The historian George Grant says that not only were abortion, infanticide, exposure, and abandonment common throughout the cultures of the world at the time of Christ, but all the intellectuals of the day saw nothing wrong with it.

> None of the great minds of the ancient world—from Plato and Aristotle to Livy and Cicero, from Herodotus and Thucydides to Plutarch and Euripides—disparaged child-killing in any way. In fact, most of them actually recommended it.[1]

Then Christ came. And the Spirit that led Him to endure the cross in obedience and raised Him from the dead filled the hearts of His followers. Immediately, Christians started to cherish and defend innocent human life.

Evidence for this arises in the very first generations of Christians. The *Didache* is one of the earliest documents we have from the Christian community. It was written about the same time that the Book of Revelation was written, around the end of the first century. Among its many instructions is a call to cherish and defend innocent human life:

There are two different ways: the way of life and the way of death, and the difference between these two ways is great. Therefore, do not murder a child by abortion or kill a newborn infant.[2]

Clement of Alexandria, Tertullian, Bishop Ambrose, Jerome—all key leaders of the early church—spoke out with vigor and consistency against the inhumanity of abortion and called on the church to stop it.

Augustine, Men, and Abortion Culpability

Augustine exposed the moral responsibility that men bear in abortion. "They provoke women to such extravagant methods as to use poisonous drugs to secure barrenness; or else, if unsuccessful in this, to murder the unborn child."[3]

Men continue to be the number one reason that women choose abortion over giving birth. Men favor abortion more than women do. A 1994 Roper poll revealed that 48 percent of men favored a more pro-abortion position, while only 40 percent of women did so. In a 1998 Writhlin poll, women consistently expressed a more pro-life position (61 percent) than did men (53 percent). According to this same poll, men were also more likely to think abortion improved male/female relationships, while the majority of women disagreed.

Consciously or unconsciously, abortion enables men to be more sexually promiscuous, since it allows for the dreaded complication of a baby to be dealt with. That is why early feminists such as Susan B. Anthony ardently opposed abortion as just another avenue for men to exploit women. "I deplore the horrible crime of child murder," she wrote, "but oh! thrice guilty is he who drove her to the desperation which impelled her."[4]

After talking to hundreds of women in pregnancy distress, and thousands more through our staff, I can assure you that men are pivotal in the abortion decision. The following young woman's anguished story is typical:

> My family would not support my decision
> to keep the baby. My boyfriend said he
> would give me no emotional or financial
> help whatsoever. All the people that mat-
> tered told me to abort. When I said I didn't
> want to, they started listing reasons why I

should. That it would have detrimental effects on my career, and my health, and that I would have no social life and no future with men. Could I actually do it alone? I started feeling like maybe I was crazy to want to keep it.

I finally told everyone that I would have the abortion…I was scared to not do it because of how my family and boyfriend felt. I'm so angry at myself for giving in to the pressure of others. I just felt so alone in my feelings to have my baby.[5]

According to Frederica Mathewes-Green in her book *Real Choices*, the highest number of women (38.2 percent) resort to abortion in response to pressure from a husband or a boyfriend.[6] Sociologist Dr. David Reardon, in his book *Aborted Women, Silent No More*, writes, "The opinions and pressures of others played a major role in the final decision of most aborting women…*nearly 55% of the respondents felt they had been very much 'forced' to abort by others*" (italics original).[7] 51 percent of the time this other person was a husband or boyfriend.[8]

Dr. Phillip Ney, a Canadian researcher of abortion's psychological effects, reports that in a first pregnancy, if a woman's partner is present but not supportive, she has a four times greater chance of having an abortion; if the partner is absent, she has a six times greater chance of aborting. During a second pregnancy, if the partner is present but unsupportive, there is a 700 percent increased chance of abortion; and if the partner is absent, there is an 1800 percent increased chance of abortion.[9]

Even when men have insisted on having the baby and promised their support, and it is the mother who is determined to have an abortion, mothers will often tell me that it is because they do not believe the father's promises. They worry that once the baby has arrived, the father will abandon his responsibilities. So even in this situation, the man is the determining factor.

Augustine long ago called upon the Christian community to intervene. If we are to do so, we must understand that abortion is primarily a *men's* movement. We must confess our own culpability for the sin of abortion. We must reach young men with a persuasive moral vision for sexuality—one that treats "young women as sisters, with absolute purity" (1 Timothy 5:2). We must incite a vision and inspire a passion in every father to provide for and protect his own children.

Basil of Caesarea, a Pastoral Example

Basil of Caesarea (329–379), the great patriarchal hero of the Greek Orthodox wing of the church, was no doubt the greatest Christian leader of his age. A teacher and biblical scholar, he wrote tracts and books in defense of orthodox Christianity and against the heresy of his day, Arianism, which denied the full humanity of Jesus. A devoted and busy pastor in a large parish church, he held 18 services a week (except for Christmas and Easter, when he led even more). He taught the youth, visited the sick, and kept up with heavy correspondence.

Basil was appalled to discover a guild of abortionists working in his city. He was also outraged. He was further horrified to learn that these abortionists were collecting fetal remains and selling them to cosmetologists in Egypt, who added them to various health and beauty creams they manufactured. All of this, including the abortion itself, was "legal."

Even worse, this was not something exceptional or rare in Roman culture. George Grant explains:

> According to the centuries old tradition of *paterfamilias*, the birth of a Roman was not a biological fact. Infants were received into the world only as the family willed. A Roman did not *have* a child; he *took* a child. Immediately after birthing, if the family decided not to raise the child—literally, lifting him above the earth—he was simply abandoned. There were special high places or walls outside most Roman cities where the newborn was taken and exposed to die.[10]

Basil responded to this inhumanity by providing pastoral leadership. He marshaled the resources of the Christian community to life-saving and life-changing action.

1. He gave a series of sermons, using Scripture to affirm the sanctity of human life and the humanity of preborn children.

2. He called upon the Christian community to stop aborting their own babies, and he called

them to actively defend innocent life by helping mothers in pregnancy distress find the help they needed to give life. In other words, he inspired the church to do the work and ministry of crisis pregnancy centers and maternity homes.

3. He launched a legislative battle using his power and influence to criminalize abortion.

4. He launched an education program to teach the entire city about the value of human life and to stigmatize and denounce abortion among the general population.

I cannot see how to improve upon this example in our own age. I can envision no appreciable success in delegitimizing and discarding abortion in our own age apart from our present-day leaders calling their churches to cherish and defend human life along the same avenues of action advocated by Basil. The battle is not new; it is just *our* turn. In Basil, we have a great example to follow.

The Emperor Valentinian, in response to Basil's work, criminalized the four evils of abortion, infanticide, exposure, and abandonment. In A.D. 374 he declared, "All parents must support their children conceived; those who brutalize or abandon them should be subject to the full penalty prescribed by law."[11]

"For the first time in human history," writes George Grant, "abortion, infanticide, exposure and abandonment were made illegitimate. The *sagae* were driven underground and eventually out of business altogether. The tradition of *paterfamilias* was all but overturned. The exposure walls were destroyed. And the high places were brought low. When Basil died just four years later, at the age of fifty, he had not only made his mark on the church, he had also altered the course of human history."[12]

Justinian and the Adoption Option

As Christian truths permeated the Western world, the pagan practices of abortion, infanticide, exposure, and abandonment continued to be denounced. In the sixth century the Emperor Justinian (483–565) discovered that the laws protecting innocent life were contradictory and nonuniform.[13] He set out to codify the right to life.

His legislation prohibited abortion and protected the victims of harsh circumstances. Adoption was passionately encouraged. He declared:

Those who expose children, possibly hoping they would die and those who use the potions of the abortionist are subject to the full penalty of the law....Should exposure occur, the finder of the child is to see that he is baptized and that he is treated with Christian care and compassion. They may be adopted as *ad scriptitiorumæ* even as we ourselves have been adopted into the kingdom of grace.[14]

Nothing seems more natural to me, as one welcomed into the family of God, than adoption. After all, besides the comparison to marriage, adoption is the most prominent point of comparison used to describe the glory of the gospel itself. Paul summarizes the gospel, saying, "Praise be to the God and Father of our Lord Jesus Christ who... predestined us to be adopted as his sons through Jesus Christ" (Ephesians 1:3, 5). John understood the joy of the gospel as emanating from God's willingness to adopt us and bestow on us the title of sons and daughters. He said, "To all who received him, to those who believed in his name, he gave the right to become children of God" (John 1:12). The Great

Commission itself (Matthew 28:18-20) is based on
the glad desire of God to adopt more and more
people and make them His very own children. No
wonder Justinian, centuries ago, thought that
adopting the "unwanted" was the most natural of
all Christian obligations.

Sadly today, the adoption option is alarm-
ingly rare among women in unplanned pregnancies. But some crisis pregnancy centers are seeing
as much as a 10 percent adoption rate among the
mothers they serve. In Boston, we have not been
nearly that successful. When our mothers do
choose adoption it is one of the most rewarding
moments in pro-life work. The birth mother and
the adoptive parents come together. Tears of sad-
ness and tears of joy flow at the same time. Each
is grateful for the other. Words are difficult to
come by. They are halting and the air is thick
with eternal hopes. Life is messy, but it is full of
glory.

The Middle Ages and the Sanctity of Human Life Sunday

During the so-called Middle Ages, the church
added the Feast of the Holy Innocents to its

liturgical calendar. Matthew 2:16 tells of Herod's anger over the birth of Christ. Hoping to eliminate this "threat" to his kingdom, Herod ordered the slaughter of all the boys in Bethlehem and the surrounding area who were two years old or younger. The wrenching grief of their mothers had been prophesied—"Rachael weeping for her children and refusing to be comforted, because they are no more" (Matthew 2:18; see Jeremiah 31:15).

By appointing the Feast of the Holy Innocents, the church sought to make sure that her leaders had occasion to remind the people to cherish and defend innocent human life.

Today, in both liturgical and nonliturgical churches, there is a growing practice of designating the third Sunday in January as Sanctity of Human Life Sunday. The date was chosen in solemn recognition that on January 22, 1973, the U.S. Supreme Court ruled that the preborn child was not a person and could be aborted for any reason or no reason. Churches of every denomination are using this annual occasion to proclaim the message of life and to inspire volunteers for the great work—defending the preborn.

John Calvin's Gospel: Defend the Innocent, Offer Hope to the Guilty

John Calvin (1509–1564), the leader of the Swiss Reformation, was passionate about defending innocent human life:

> The unborn child…though enclosed in the womb of its mother, is already a human being…and should not be robbed of the life which it has not yet begun to enjoy. If it seems more horrible to kill a man in his own house than in a field, because a man's house is his place of most secure refuge, it ought surely to be deemed more atrocious to destroy an unborn child in the womb before it has come to light.[15]

He called on the church to be as diligent and devoted to the preservation of the innocent as they were to the preservation and dissemination of the gospel message to the guilty. He called them to suffer for both, if need be.

> I say that not only they that labor for the defense of the gospel, but they that in any

way maintain the cause of righteousness, suffer persecution for righteousness. Therefore, whether declaring God's truth against Satan's falsehoods or in taking up the protection of the good and innocent against the wrongs of the wicked, we must undergo the offenses and hatred of the world, which may imperil either our life, our fortunes or our honor.[16]

Ignatius Loyola's Resolve

Ignatius Loyola (1491–1556) was one of the most prominent leaders of the Catholic Reformation during the same time that Calvin was calling for reforms. He called the church to face the truth of abortion squarely and to resolve to do something about it.

> Life is God's most precious gift. Abortion…is not merely an awful tyranny, it is a smear against the integrity of God as well. Suffer as we must, even die if need be, such rebellion against heaven must not be free to run its terrible courses.[17]

Vincent de Paul's Reminder that God's Commands Are Not Burdensome

In Paris, the pastor Vincent de Paul led his church to demonstrate their commitment to holding each life precious by launching special ministries to help galley slaves, abandoned elderly, unwanted children, and convicts. In 1652, de Paul learned of a guild of abortionists operating in the slums of Paris. Vincent took to his pulpit to sound a clear trumpet on the demands made on those who claimed to follow the law of love.

He reminded the people that pro-life work was mandatory; the church is commanded to rescue the innocent. He also reminded them that God's commands are not burdensome; rather, they are profoundly fulfilling:

> When'ere God's people gather, there is life in the midst of them—yea, Christ's gift to us as a people is life, and that more abundantly. To protect the least of these, our brethren is not merely facultative, it is exigent. In addition though, it is among the greatest and most satisfying of our sundry stewardships.[18]

William Carey, Missionary to the Innocent
Kenneth Scott Latourette, the famous church historian, called the nineteenth century the Glorious Century. For Protestants, it is the age of modern missions. The father of this movement is William Carey (1761–1834). He is famous for his creed, *Expect great things from God, attempt great things for God.*

Raised as a shoe cobbler, Carey left England to bring the gospel to India. He spent 40 years there. Modern India owes much to the passion, humility, innovation, and commitment to life that Carey brought with him.

Vishal and Ruth Mangalwadi, in their book *The Legacy of William Carey,* outline the remarkable contributions he made to modern India.[19] They point out that Carey was a botanist. One of three varieties of eucalyptus found only in India is named after him: *Careya Herbacea.* According to Carey's gospel, all of creation is good and points to the glory of God. He published the first books on natural history in India to stress that "all thy works praise Thee, O Lord."

Carey was an industrialist. He helped introduce the steam engine to India and was the first to produce indigenous paper for printing and publishing books.

Carey was an economist. Believing that God hated usury, and seeing the pervasive and impoverishing effects of loans with interest rates from 36 to 72 percent, Carey introduced the idea of savings banks to India.

Carey was a publisher. He brought the modern science of printing and publishing to India. He established the first newspaper ever printed in any Oriental language, because according to Carey's gospel, "Above all forms of truth and faith, Christianity seeks free discussion."

Carey was an astronomer. He introduced the science and mathematics of astronomy to India. Since God created the world and set men to rule it, heavenly bodies were not deities. They could be measured, charted, and counted. The science of astronomy, Carey recognized, would topple the fatalism and superstitious fear sown by astrology.

Carey was a translator and educator. He started dozens of schools for Indian children of all castes. He started the first college in Asia, at Serampore near Calcutta. He rose to become a professor of languages.

Above all, Carey was a missionary. His desire was to bring the gospel to the people. He started by translating the Bible into Bengali, Sanskrit, and Marathi. He wrote two grammars and a dictionary. After 19 years of work, a fire struck and all these manuscripts were destroyed. Carey bowed before Almighty God and started all over again!

By the end of his life, he had translated and published the Bible or parts of it into 36 languages and dialects; started schools and hospitals; founded Serampore College; and opened numerous medical clinics.

But the same gospel that led him to do all this never allowed him to be silent when innocent blood was being shed. He saw missionary work as both preaching salvation *and* protecting the innocent and the weak. The law of love compelled both.

Upon arriving in India he learned that abortion, infanticide, exposure, and abandonment were part of the way of life. One day he "came across a basket suspended from a tree. Inside were the remains of an infant which had been exposed; only the skull was left, the rest having been devoured by white ants."[20] When he moved to Serampore, he discovered that over 100 babies were "sacrificed" every year, thrown into the Ganges River, where they were eaten by alligators. "This was looked upon as a most holy sacrifice—giving the Mother Ganges the fruit of their bodies for the sons of their souls."[21]

Carey launched an all-out effort to stop this ritual of child sacrifice. He was accused of imposing his moral values on others. Yet this practice was eventually outlawed. And the pro-life legislation that was eventually passed is called to this very day Carey's Edict.

Amy Carmichael's Enormous Fuss

One hundred years later, the missionary Amy Carmichael (1867–1951) arrived in southern India. She learned that "the sale of children as temple prostitutes to be 'married to the gods' and then made available to Hindu men who frequented the temple was one of the 'secret sins' of Hinduism."[22] When a seven-year-old girl ran away from such a cult temple, Amy, following the law of love, took her in and refused to return her. In defending this innocent life, Amy offended the acceptable, legal practices of her time. Nonetheless, her actions declared, "Not on my watch!"

For refusing to accept the destruction of innocent life, she was harshly criticized by the government. She was even charged with kidnapping on several occasions! In her own words, saving this one innocent child "created an enormous fuss."[23] But she continued to rescue the innocent, and 12 years later, she had 139 young girls under her care.

The historian Ruth Tucker adds:

> The children were educated and physically cared for, special attention was paid to the development of their 'Christian character.' To critics who charged that her emphasis on physical needs, education and character-building was not evangelistic enough, Amy responded: "…one cannot save and then pitchfork souls into heaven…Souls are more or less securely fastened to bodies…and as you cannot get the souls out and deal with them separately, you have to take them both together."[24]

Her message, the message of the gospel, authenticated by courage and care, spread rapidly through the region.

Harriet Tubman and the Underground Railroad

Harriet Tubman (1820–1913) orchestrated the rescue of hundreds of runaway slaves out of her home in Philadelphia through the Underground Railroad. The historical parallels to the present test are remarkable. Abortion and slavery both required a Supreme Court decision. The Dred Scott case (1857) ruled that blacks were not persons worthy of protection under the Constitution. Roe v. Wade (1973) ruled the same for preborn children. The slave, like the preborn child, was considered private property. Presenting slave ownership as a "privacy" issue, proponents argued that they did not want to impose their religion on others. Slavery was a matter of choice. Pro-abortionists argue today: If you don't like abortion, don't have one. Inherent in that slogan is the notion that moral opposition to abortion is tolerable as long as you do not try to impose it on others.

Newton's Pulpit and Wilberforce's Parliament

In England the slave trade, fully legal and institutionalized, was attacked by a hundred Christian men from pulpits to the Parliament. "Humanity is a private feeling, not a public principle to act upon," protested the Earl of Abington. Lord Melborne decried the rising voices of pastors who preached the sanctity of human life and decried the inhumanity of slavery. "Things have come to a pretty pass when religion is allowed to invade public life."[25]

Reverend John Newton was one of the people he probably had in mind. Newton was a former captain of a "slaver" ship. He knew better than anyone the inhumanity of the slave trade. After his conversion, he left that "business" and made his way into the Anglican Church as a preacher. He was a living example that God loves the guilty and is willing to forgive the repentant. His hymn "Amazing Grace" is one of the most enduring hymns of church history.

But Newton also knew that God loved the innocent as well, and he called upon His people to "speak up for those who cannot speak for themselves." He wrote a pamphlet exposing the vile inhumanity of the slave trade. He testified before legislators. He taught from the Scriptures the sanctity of all human life.

One man who heard him was William Wilberforce. As a member of Parliament, Wilberforce labored for 20 years to abolish the slave trade (1787–1807). Having succeeded, he labored another 26 years to abolish slavery itself. On July 26, 1833, slavery was outlawed in Britain and human rights for blacks were secured. Three days later Wilberforce died.

In a remarkable historic parallel, God has transformed most of the key leaders that led to the legalization of abortion in America. Bernard Nathanson, mentioned earlier as the abortionist who helped plan the legal effort to legalize abortion nationwide, came to faith in Christ in 1996 (see Notes, chapter 5, #7). Like Newton, Nathanson, in his book *The Hand of God*, writes of his amazement at the grace of God who can forgive "sinners." He continues to write and speak with a painful eloquence, calling the nation to cherish and defend innocent preborn life.

Norma McCorvey is the "Jane Roe" of the infamous "Roe v. Wade" Supreme Court decision. To cover up an affair in 1969, Norma lied about her pregnancy, saying she was raped. Two feminist lawyers recruited her to become America's test case on abortion. She herself never had an abortion, but her case nullified all restrictions on abortion in America.

In 1995, Operation Rescue, the group that organized nonviolent sit-ins outside abortion facilities, opened an office next door to the abortion clinic where Norma was employed. Several encounters outside their offices during lunch hour softened her heart. When eight-year-old Emily Mackey, the daughter of a pro-life volunteer, asked Norma to attend church with her, she agreed. That night she gave her life to Christ. She was baptized later that year. The *New York Post* headline said, "Jane Roe Flip-Flops on Abortion" and underneath screamed, "I'M PRO-LIFE." Since her conversion, she too has devoted her life to defending the innocent as well as proclaiming forgiveness to all.[26]

If we follow the law of love, one day, as a nation, we will look back on abortion the way we currently look back on slavery. As we courageously speak up and wisely direct God's people toward compassionate intervention, we should go forward recalling the timeless words of William Wilberforce:

> Never, never will we desist till we…extinguish every trace of this bloody traffic, of which our posterity, looking back to the history of these enlightened times, will scarce believe that it has been suffered to exist so long a disgrace and dishonor to this country.[27]

/ NINE /

Whatever Happened to…

The young, sweet-voiced 16-year-old who called my office (see chapter 2), so immobilized by fear of pregnancy that she threatened suicide and so clear about the evil of taking a human life that she would never be able to live with herself afterward, never came into our center. I never heard from her again and do not know what happened to her. But I remember her voice daily that I might be ready to reach others.

The couple who came in with nine of their 10 children in tow had a happier ending. While the rambunctious children tore the office apart, we adults talked through the abortion question. At one point I asked the father to consider the following: "If money is the issue, and you cannot afford 11 children, why not kill your 15-year-old and save the 15-week-old preborn child? You will save *much more* money. After all, teenagers eat more, they want $200 sneakers and a college degree." He laughed at the proposal and translated it to his wife. She did not laugh and neither did I. We both understood the point. The father said nervously, "We can't do that." I agreed, "No matter what financial problems we face, killing our children is not a solution." He said, "I understand. Of course you are right." He told his wife that abortion is not the answer. She began to cry *with joy!*

This immigrant mother would have been devastated by an abortion. Her lifelong mission was loving and raising her children. Providentially, a local church had held a "diaper drive," where everyone comes to church with a package of diapers to give away to new mothers. Church members had delivered several huge plastic bags filled with dozens of such packages to our office. I gave them all to this family of 10, with one on the way.

"This is a down payment," I told them, "on the promise that those who trust in God will not go hungry."

In the weeks that followed, Christians in their hometown offered this father work. They assisted the family with clothes and other baby materials. Some months later they returned with their baby. It is tough to raise 10 kids; but it is not measurably tougher raising 11. Things work out.

The postgraduate student went on to have her baby. The father, who threatened my life because I was "ruining his life," came to see that, indeed, having a baby and becoming a father was a great blessing. He became very excited about the baby. When we prepared a layette of goods for them (which we give to all our new mothers), she came by to pick it up and to thank us. I was hoping to greet the father, but he told his wife he was too embarrassed by his past behavior to come and see me. I sent word that I was happy for him and would welcome a visit anytime.

The daughters of the three local pastors went on to have their babies. Two of them married. By the time the baby came, the daughter who was so hurt and angered worked out her hurt and disappointment with her father. They figured out what the law of love demanded of them both, and when her son was born, she named him after her father.

What happened to "X", the one who was a senior at a local Christian college? She was about to abort her faith as well as her baby. She had been told by the abortion facility that she was 14 weeks pregnant and that her abortion would cost $750. She called our center, looking for a better price. She ended up kneeling and recommitting her life to Jesus Christ in our counseling room. She decided to trust that God could forgive her and that God would take care of her and her baby. We paid for her initial prenatal care visit. The day after, the doctor called and asked me if I was sitting down. I sat down and the doctor said, "She isn't pregnant!"

This beautiful young woman had gone into the abortion facility in a state of panic. She was racked with guilt over behavior she did not believe was proper. They sold her an abortion and scheduled an appointment for her to return once she found the money. Had she not come to my office, she never would have known *that she wasn't even pregnant.* Her story is one reason many pregnancy help centers now offer ultrasound verification and even prenatal care.

For the couple who came in, admitting a background of drugs and alcoholism, unemployed and both married to someone else, it was a difficult case. The baby arrived and, eventually, with the help of many Christians doing a small part to help, they made it through several years of instability.

Some mothers go on to place their child for adoption. Some marry. Some learn from their mistakes, and others repeat them again and again. In each case, we ask ourselves, what does love require of us in this situation? Then we seek to follow that course, simply and directly, with the aid of the Christian community.

TEN

Final Appeal to Pastors

Unless your local church consists only of very old people and lacks any evangelistic thrust, you have postaborted men and women in your church. In mine it turned out to be about 30 percent. As the testimonies of women and couples revealed, this sin so stained their conscience that many struggled with whether God could or should really forgive them.

Those involved in the care of souls, those who have a passion for evangelism, those seeking to equip and send out strong and confident Christians into a troubled world, need to recognize that abortion, and the bloodguilt it invokes, must be dealt with authoritatively. The silence of the pulpit only adds to their condemnation. The message sent is that this sin is so horrific that we cannot address it. And perversely, silence for those who, at that moment, are frightened and embarrassed by pregnancy, is interpreted to mean approval of abortion. "If it was really the killing of a child, surely the pastor would denounce it wholeheartedly and regularly and the church would be organized to offer hope and help in this situation."

Permit a dyed-in-the-wool Baptist minister to quote Pope John Paul II once more. He says it so well:

> Where life is involved, the service of charity must be profoundly consistent....Newborn life is served by centers of assistance and homes where new life receives a welcome. Thanks to the work of such centers, many unmarried mothers and couples in difficulty discover hope and find assistance and support in overcoming hardship and the fear of accepting a newly conceived life.[1]

Among evangelicals, many leaders have voiced similar calls for the church to partner with local centers that aid and assist mothers in pregnancy distress. Unless our leaders speak up and guide the church in this direction, the church will remain passive and self-absorbed. Author and pastor Chuck Swindoll wrote:

> Of all the issues I have encountered through all the years I have been engaged in people-related involvements, none are more significant than the sanctity of life and sexual purity. The groundswell of concern surrounding each has made them the inescapable issues of our times. Remaining silent on either is no longer an option.[2]

May God help us follow the law of love and so become the "aroma of life."

How You Can H.E.L.P. (Hold Each Life Precious)

1. Start with getting a clean conscience and a heart for life. For those of us with deeply stained consciences concerning abortion, a God-pleasing, soul-satisfying, conscience-cleansing, fresh experience of the forgiveness of God through faith in the cross of Jesus Christ is needed before anything else can be done.

For confidential help in dealing with the personal impact of abortion, contact Ramah International at 941.473.2188 or go online to www.ramahinternational.org.

In addition, most pregnancy help centers provide:

- Post-abortion counseling and Bible-studies on forgiveness.
- Training on how to start a ministry in your church to men and women struggling with abortion guilt.

To understand the effects of abortion, go online to www.afterabortion.org and www. abortionbreast cancer.com.

Additional Web sites of pro-life organizations: Baptists for Life (www.bfl.org), Care Net (www. care-net.org), Christian Life Resources (www. christianliferesources.com), Heartbeat International (www.heartbeatinternational.org), International Life Services, Inc. (www.life-services. org), National Institute of Family Life Advocates (www.nifla.org), National Life Center (www. Nationallifecenter.com), North American Mission Board (www.namb.net), Sav-A-Life (www. savalife.org).

2. Learn what to say to someone considering abortion. Remember, God's love may require you to get involved. When this happens, use the LOVE approach:

L   Listen and learn. Let her tell her story. It is probably full of embarrassment, regret, anger, fears, confusion, and urgency. An unplanned pregnancy feels like death (her life as she projected it is dying due to the pregnancy). Listen till you understand this.

O   Open options. Women most often turn to abortion believing they have "no choice." Remind her that this is untrue: She does have a choice. Help her explore the dangers and opportunities that each of her choices offer.

V   Vision and value. Help her to see that pregnancy is not the end of her life, just a chapter in life. Her future plans may be delayed or changed entirely, but often life's unexpected challenges produce in us our greatest sources of pride and self-fulfillment.

E   Extend and enable. Help her plan her immediate steps, and help her take them, if needed. Help her prepare in the coming weeks and months for parenting or adoption.

This is an abbreviated summary of a training manual, *Planting the Seed: The Love Approach*, by Dr. Margaret Hartshorn, president of Heartbeat International (used by permission). All new volunteers and staff working at local pregnancy help centers receive this or similar training.

3. Help bring ultrasound and medical service to your pregnancy help center. Sacrificial and generous giving over these next few years will allow pregnancy help centers to expand their services to include ultrasound services and a consultation with a medical professional. Ultrasound, in the hands of caring, articulate Christian medical doctors, nurses, and sonographers, may soon help women reject abortion in numbers that endanger the financial stability of the abortion industry.

In Boston, in our first year of using ultrasound, medical professionals working at A Woman's Concern pregnancy health centers saw the rate of women choosing life go up from 35 percent to 76 percent. A total of 329 women were spared abortions in the first 18 months of operation, with an estimated cost to the abortion industry of $148,500. Your treasure invested in a pregnancy help center, when combined with others', will make abortion unprofitable and unnecessary long before it will become unlawful.

Special note to Christian medical professionals! You hold the key to helping women and couples understand the humanity of their preborn children as well as sparing roughly 20 percent of women, who have nonviable pregnancies and will naturally miscarry by eight weeks, from having abortions at six weeks.

To learn about the dramatic impact that ultrasound is making go online to www.awomans concern.org/partners.

To learn how you can assist pregnancy help centers provide medical services, contact the National Institute for Family and Life Advocates at 540.785.9853 or go online to www.nifla.org.

To learn how Christian medical professionals are coming together to transform the medical culture, contact the Physicians Life Alliance at 501.521.0105 or go online to www.physicians lifealliance.org.

4. Volunteer your time and talents to the pregnancy help center in your area. Typically each one is looking for help in the following areas:

Professional Services: doctor, nurse, radiologist, sonographer, medical management, L.S.W.

Counseling Services: peer counselor, hotline counselor, crisis intervention, abstinence educator.

Client Support: client advocate/mentor, post-abortion classes, parenting classes.

Administration: receptionist, accounting, data entry, receipting, bulk mailing, IT support

Development: banquet committee, donor relations, publications, grant writing.

5. Pray. Pray that the same courageous and compassionate spirit that has moved the church throughout the ages to cherish and defend innocent human life will lay hold of this present generation of Christians in ever-increasing numbers and with dramatic results. Pray for the 3,000 neighborhood pregnancy help centers working daily to assist women and couples in pregnancy distress. Most have them have made the following Commitment of Care that makes them especially worthy of your unceasing intercession.

The Commitment of Care

- Clients are served without regard to age, race, income, nationality, religious affiliation, disability, or other arbitrary circumstances.

- Clients are treated with kindness, compassion, and in a caring manner.
- Clients always receive honest and open answers.
- Client pregnancy tests are distributed and administered in accordance with all applicable laws.
- Client information is held in strict and absolute confidence. Client information is only disclosed as required by law and when necessary to protect the client or others against imminent harm.
- Clients receive accurate information about pregnancy, fetal development, lifestyle issues, and related concerns.
- We do not offer, recommend, or refer for abortions or abortifacients, but we are committed to offering accurate information about abortion procedures and risks.
- All of our advertising and communications are truthful and honest and accurately describe the services we offer.
- All of our staff and volunteers receive proper training to uphold these standards.

/ Notes /

Chapter 1

1. Quoted from a Focus on the Family radio spot produced for crisis pregnancy centers.

Chapter 2

1. Pope John Paul II, *The Gospel of Life* (New York: Random House, 1995), pp. 4, 22.

2. From the foreword to *Operation Rescue,* by Randall Terry (Springfield, Pa: Whitaker House, 1988).

3. Peter Singer, "Taking Human Life," in *Practical Ethics* 2nd ed. (New York: Cambridge University Press, 1993). Singer is not alone. Francis Crick and James Watson, who won the Nobel prize for the discovery of the double-helix structure of DNA, advocate that all newborns who fail a health test be euthanized (see C. Everett Koop, "Life and Death and the Handicapped Unborn," *Issues in Law and Medicine 5,* no. 1 [June 22, 1989], p. 101). Steven Pinker of MIT, asserting that humans are ever evolving, calls for acceptance of "neonaticide" as natural selection in process

(see Steven Pinker, "Why They Kill Their New-borns," *The New York Times,* November 2, 1997).

It is not uncommon for us to read newspaper accounts of newborn babies thrown in trash cans or toilets. This is abortion rights extended to its natural next step. As a result, some pregnancy help centers are establishing themselves as drop-off zones for babies who might otherwise be abandoned.

4. Don Feder of the *Boston Herald* reported in 1997 that FBI records report 207 babies less than a week old murdered in 1994, a 92 percent increase since 1973.

5. In 1976 there were 669,000 cases of child abuse reported in the U.S. In 1994, there were 2.9 million cases reported.

6. Dr. Anne Speckhard, in her study "The Psycho-Social Aspects of Stress Following Abortion," concluded that 65 percent of women have thoughts of suicide following an abortion. Another study concluded, "The suicide rate after an abortion was three times the general suicide rate" (see "Study Links Abortion, Risk of Suicide," *The Boston Globe*, December 6, 1996, p. A13).

Chapter 3

1. For a comprehensive overview of the 1973 Roe v. Wade and Doe v. Bolton rulings, see www.roevwade.org.

2. Alan Guttmacher Institute, "Induced Abortion," *Facts in Brief,* February 2002. This fact sheet says, "The data in this fact sheet are the most current available. Most are from research conducted by the Alan Guttmacher Institute. An additional source is the Centers for Disease Control and Prevention."

3. David Reardon, *Aborted Women, Silent No More* (Chicago: Loyola University Press, 1997), p. xi.

4. For a full treatment of abortion sequelae, see David Reardon's book *Aborted Women, Silent No More.* See also www.afterabortion.org.

5. Alan Guttmacher Institute, "Induced Abortion," *Facts in Brief,* January 1998.

6. "Strong Ties Between Religious Commitment and Abortion Views," *Gallup Poll Monthly,* April 1993, pp. 35-43. See also "Abortion Patients in 1994-1995: Characteristics and Contraceptive Use," *Family Planning Perspectives,* vol. 28, no. 4 (July/August 1996).

7. For a fuller treatment of guilt and forgiveness, see John Ensor, *Experiencing God's Forgiveness: The*

Journey from Guilt to Gladness (Colorado Springs: NavPress, 1997).

8. Available through Easton Publishing Company. See www.eastonpublishing.com.

9. Centers for Disease Control and Prevention, *Morbidity and Mortality Weekly Report, Abortion Surveillance,* CDC Surveillance Summaries, August 8, 1997. MMWR 1997; 46 (No. SS-4)

10. Alan Guttmacher Institute, "The Limitations of U.S. Statistics on Abortion," *Facts in Brief,* January 1997. See also Aida Torres and J. D. Forrest, "Why Do Women Have Abortions?" *Family Planning Perspectives* 20, no. 4 (July/August 1988), p. 170.

11. Barbara Carton, "The Dollars and Cents of the Abortion Business," *Wall Street Journal,* January 16, 1995, B-1.

12. "Abortion Attitudes in the African American Community," the Center for Business and Economic Research (University of Dayton). The research was commissioned by Dayton Right to Life. Found at www.dayton.right to life.org/news.

13. Stanley Henshaw and Kathryn Kost, *Family Planning Perspectives,* July/August 1996. Volume 28, No. 4.

14. 1994 Roper poll.
15. Centers for Disease Control and Prevention, *Morbidity and Morality Weekly Report, Abortion Surveillance: Priminary Analysis*—United States, 1989, Nov. 29, 1991; 40 (No. 47), pp. 817-818.

Chapter 4

1. The information in this section and much of the information under the church history section come from George Grant's excellent book *Third Time Around: The History of the Pro-Life Movement from the First Century to the Present* (Brentwood, Tenn.: Wolgemuth & Hyatt, 1991).
2. *Third Time Around*, p. 15.
3. John Jefferson Davis, *Abortion and the Christian* (Phillipsburg, N.J.: Presbyterian and Reformed Publishing, 1984), p. 40.
4. Clifford Bajema, *Abortion and the Meaning of Personhood* (Grand Rapids: Baker Book House, 1974), p. 32.

Chapter 5

1. Quoted from Randy Alcorn, *ProLife Answers to ProChoice Arguments* (Portland: Multnomah,

1992), p. 41. For additional references from embryology textbooks, see pages 40-42.

2. John Stott, *Christianity Today*, September 5, 1980, p. 50.

In recent years, those involved in marketing combination oral contraceptives ("the pill") and in promoting the so-called "morning after pill" have argued that life begins not at conception but at implantation. This is overtly erroneous and misleading. The reason for positing this notion is marketing. They are trying to make the pill, the most commonly used form of contraceptive, acceptable to those who reject abortion. According to the manufacturers, the pill works in three ways. First, it suppresses ovulation (the release of an egg from the ovary), thus preventing conception. Second, it thickens the cervical mucus, making it harder for the sperm to reach the egg if, in fact, ovulation has occurred (again preventing conception). The third mechanism of the pill is to affect the lining of the womb (the endometrium) so that implantation (of a newly conceived human life) is impossible. In such cases the newly conceived baby is unable to receive nourishment from the mother and is expelled. This is a chemical abortion. See R. A.

Hatcher et al., *Contraceptive Technology* (New York: Irving Publishers, 1990), p. 228. See also Randy Alcorn, *Does the Birth Control Pill Cause Abortions?* (Gresham, OR: Eternal Perspectives Ministries, 2000). Also online at www.epm.org/bcp.html.

3. Keith L. Moore, *The Developing Human*, 4th ed. (Philadelphia: Saunders Co, 1988), p. 329. I am indebted to the National Right to Life Web site for a compilation of most the information included here on embryology. See www.nrlc.org.

4. According to the *Morbidity and Mortality Weekly Report* of the Centers for Disease Control and Prevention. 43, no. 50 (December 23, 1994), p. 931, only 13.8 percent of abortions are performed prior to seven weeks of gestation.

5. Roe v. Wade declares that the state may limit late-term abortions in the interest of protecting fetal life after viability, "except when it is necessary to preserve the life or health of the mother." Doe v. Bolton, the Supreme Court decision handed down with Roe v. Wade, defined the health of the mother to be "the physical, emotional, psychological, familial and the woman's age…all these factors may relate to health."

The U.S. Senate Judiciary Committee con-

cluded in an official report (Report #98-149) after
extensive hearings in 1982: "No significant legal
barriers of any kind whatsoever exist today in the
United States for a woman to obtain an abortion
for any reason during any stage of her pregnancy."

6. "Q & A with Bernard Nathanson" *Focus on the
   Family Citizen* magazine, August 26, 1996, p. 7.

7. Bernard Nathanson, *The Hand of God* (Washington:
   Regnery Publishing, 1996), p. 19. Ultrasound led
   Nathanson to renounce abortion and become a
   staunch defender of the rights of preborn children. Over the years, this brought him into contact with many Christians and Christian writers.
   In 1989, he went to observe a peaceful sit-in by
   Christians in Operation Rescue. In his own
   words:

   "Now I had not been immune to the religious
   fervor of the pro-life movement. I had been aware
   in the early and mid-eighties that a great many of
   the Catholics and Protestants in the ranks had
   prayed for me, were praying for me, and I was not
   unmoved as time wore on. But it was not until I
   saw the spirit put to the test on those bitterly cold
   demonstration mornings, with pro-choicers hurl-
   ing the most fulsome epithets at them, the police

surrounding them, the media openly unsympathetic to their cause, the federal judiciary fining and jailing them, and the municipal officials threatening them—all through it they sat smiling, quietly praying, singing, confident and righteous of their cause and ineradicably persuaded of the ultimate triumph—that I began seriously to question what indescribable Force generated them to this activity. Why, too, was I there? What had led me to this time and place? Was it the same Force that allowed them to sit serene and unafraid at the epicenter of legal, physical, ethical and moral chaos?" (p. 193).

In 1996, Dr. Nathanson was baptized into the Christian faith.

8. See "Maternal Bonding in Early Fetal Ultrasound," *The New England Journal of Medicine*, February 17, 1983.

9. Paul Zielbauer, "Princeton Bioethics Professor Debates Views on Disabilities and Euthanasia," *The New York Times*, October 13, 1999, p. B8.

10. Sir Charles Bell, *The Hand: Its Mechanism and Vital Endowments as Evincing Design*, 4th ed. (London: William Pickering, 1834).

Chapter 6

1. Kim Flodin, "Why I Don't March," My Turn, *Newsweek,* February 12, 1990 p.8.

Chapter 7

1. Pope John Paul II, *The Gospel of Life, Evangelism Vitae* (New York: Random House, 1995), p. 70.
2. Virginia Ramey Mollenkott, "Reproductive Choice: Basic to Justice for Women," *Christian Scholar's Review* 17, March 1988, p. 291.
3. Anger, grief, and a natural longing to help victims of rape and incest create a false sense that women in such painful circumstances are aided by abortion. In fact, abortion in cases of rape and incest is extremely damaging to women. Researcher David Reardon concluded, "As with other 'psychological indications for abortion,' the evidence actually shows that rape is a strong contraindication for abortion" (David C. Reardon, *Aborted Women, Silent No More*, Chicago: Loyola University Press, 1997, p. 192).

Why this is so becomes clear when the trauma of rape is understood. As Dr. Reardon explains, "Victims of rape feel dirty, guilty, sexually violated, of low self-esteem, angry, fearful or hateful toward men. She may experience sexual dysfunction, she may feel she has lost control of her life. Now let's look at the symptoms of abortion. The woman feels dirty, guilty, sexually violated, of low self-esteem, angry, fearful or hateful toward men. She may experience sexual dysfunction, she may feel she has lost control of her life. All the same symptoms. Some women have described the abortion experience as feeling like rape—a form of surgical rape. Abortion then is a 'cure' that only aggravates the problem" ("The Abortion Experience for Victims of Rape and Incest," *Association for Interdisciplinary Research Newsletter*, 2, no. 1, fall 1988, pp. 4-6).

Incest victims face the same dilemma. People uncomfortable with or unwilling to address the special needs of a woman in this situation offer abortion as the only solution, masking their own discomfort in dealing with the trauma. Ultimately, abortion serves the selfish interests of the incestuous relative/perpetrator—namely, by destroying the unborn child who is tangible evidence of his evil acts. Edith Young was a rape and incest victim at age 12. She writes, "I was being sexually attacked, threatened by him and betrayed by Mom's silence....The abortion which was to be in 'my best interest' has not been...it only saved their reputations, solved their problems and allowed their lives to go merrily on" (*Aborted Women, Silent No More*, p. 217).

In 1990, a Baltimore court sentenced a man to 30 years in prison for raping his three daughters over a nine-year period. During the trial, it was revealed that the continual rape of these three girls resulted in 10 pregnancies and 10 abortions! How much better would it have been if the first pregnancy had continued. The incestuous father would have been exposed and sent to jail. The first victim would have been protected from continual sexual assault and her sisters spared altogether. The damage of 10 abortions would have been prevented and the blood of 10 children created in God's image would not have been shed. Abortion is to an incestuous male what a getaway car is to a bank robber: part of the escape plan. Abortion is never in a woman's best interest or an aid to her long-term well-being. God never asks us to violate the Ten Commandments in order to be whole and healthy.

4. Ethel Waters and Charles Samuels, *His Eye Is on the Sparrow* (Westport, Conn.: Greenwood, 1978).

5. What about abortion to "save the life" of the mother? First, it must be noted that abortion as a medically indicated solution to save a woman's life has become extremely rare, thanks to the advances made in medicine over the past 30 years. Dr. C. Everett Koop, former surgeon general of the United States and noted pediatric surgeon, stated, "Never once did a case come across my practice where abortion was necessary to save a mother's life" (quoted in Bill Hybels's book *One Church's Answer to Abortion* [Chicago: Moody Press, 1986], pp. 22-23). Dr. Thomas Murphy Goodwin, a professor of obstetrics and gynecology at the University of Southern California's Women's Hospital, has noted that many doctors are "medicalizing" abortion decisions for reasons of liability, not health care (see "Medicalizing Abortion Decisions," *First Things*, March 1996). But still, we may acknowledge the real dilemma of medical conditions associated with risk of maternal mortality. In such cases, the sanctity of human life ethic calls for the best treatment for both patients to be provided.

For a good understanding of this, see Dr. J. C. Wilke, "The Life of the Mother: Is It Needed in Legislation?" *Life Issues Connector,* July 2000. See at www.lifeissues.org/connector/00jul.html.

6. Quoted from Francis Schaeffer, *The Great Evangelical Disaster* (Eastbourne U.K.: Kingsway Publications, 1985), p. 51.

7. Eva Fogalman, *Conscience and Courage: Rescuers of Jews During the Holocaust* (New York: Anchor Books, 1994), p. 70.

8. Corrie ten Boom, *The Hiding Place* (New York: Bantam Books, 1974), p. 99.

9. Quoted from Edward, Duke of Windsor, *A King's Story: Memoirs of the Duke of Windsor* (New York: G.P. Putnam's Sons, 1951).

Chapter 8

1. George Grant, *Third Time Around: A History of the Pro-Life Movement from the First Century to the Present* (Brentwood, TN: Wolgemuth & Hyatt Publishers, Inc., 1991), p. 12.

2. Clayton Jefford, ed., *The Didache in Context, Essays on Its Test, History and Transmission* (Leiden, The Netherlands: E.J. Brill, 1995), 1.1; 2.2.

3. Aurelius Augustine, Bishop of Hippo, *On Marriage and Concupiscence*, A.D. 419–20, 1.17.15.

4. Susan B. Anthony, *The Revolution*, (New York, July 8, 1869), Vol. I, No. IV, p.4.

5. *Aborted Women, Silent No More*, p. 31.

6. Frederica Mathewes-Green, *Real Choices: Offering Practical, Life-Affirming Alternatives to Abortion* (Sisters, Oregon: Multnomah Books, 1994), p. 248.

7. *Aborted Women, Silent No More*, p. 11.

8. Ibid.

9. P. G. Ney, T. Fung, A. R. Wickett, and C. Beaman-Dodd, "The Effects of Pregnancy Loss on Women's Health," *Journal of Science and Medicine* 38 (1994), pp. 1193-1200.

10. *Aborted Women, Silent No More*, p. 20.

11. Emperor Valentinian, *The Code of Justinian*, 8.52.2.

12. *Third Time Around*, p. 21. The *sagae*, latin for "sorceress", is Grant's characterization of the women who traded on the fears of pregnant women by selling abortion services.

13. Remember that today a man and woman can kill their baby through abortion. Yet if the preborn

baby is killed in a car accident by a drunk driver, the driver can be charged with fetal homicide.

14. *Third Time Around,* p. 38.
15. John Calvin, *Calvin's Commentaries,* trans. Charles Bingham (Grand Rapids: Baker Book House, 1981), 3:42.
16. John Calvin, in "The Sum of the Christian Life: The Denial of Ourselves," trans. John T. McNeil, *The Institutes of the Christian Religion,* The Four-Volume Classroom Edition (Philadelphia: Westminster Press, 1962), p. 348.
17. *Third Time Around,* p. 59.
18. Ibid., p. 53.
19. Vishal and Ruth Mangalwadi, *The Legacy of William Carey: A Model for the Transformation of a Culture* (Wheaton: Crossway Books, 1993), pp. 17-25.
20. *The Third Time Around,* p. 148.
21. *The Legacy of William Carey,* p. 33.
22. Ruth Tucker, *From Jerusalem to Irian Jaya* (Grand Rapids: Zondervan Publishing House, 1983), p. 240.
23. Elisabeth Elliot, *Amy Carmichael* (Grand Rapids: Zondervan Publishing House, 1983), p. 169.

24. *From Jerusalem to Irian Jaya,* p. 241.
25. Quoted from Charles Colson, *Kingdoms in Conflict* (Grand Rapids: William Morrow and Zondervan Publications, 1987), p. 101.
26. Norma McCorvey's story is available on video. See *Reversing Roe: The Norma McCorvey Story.*
27. *Kingdoms in Conflict,* p. 102.

Chapter 10
1. Pope John Paul II, *The Gospel of Life,* pp. 156-157.
2. Charles Swindoll, *The Sanctity of Life* (Dallas: Word Publishing, 1990), p. xiv.

FOCUS ON THE FAMILY®

Welcome to the Family!

Whether you received this book as a gift, borrowed it from a friend, or purchased it yourself, we're glad you read it! It's just one of the many helpful, insightful, and encouraging resources produced by Focus on the Family.

In fact, that's what Focus on the Family is all about—providing inspiration, information, and biblically based advice to people in all stages of life.

It began in 1977 with the vision of one man, Dr. James Dobson, a licensed psychologist and author of 16 best-selling books on marriage, parenting, and family. Alarmed by the societal, political, and economic pressures that were threatening the existence of the American family, Dr. Dobson founded Focus on the Family with one employee—an assistant—and a once-a week radio broadcast, aired on only 36 stations.

Now an international organization, Focus on the Family is dedicated to preserving Judeo-Christian values and strengthening the family through more than 70 different ministries, including eight separate daily radio broadcasts; television public service announcements; 10 publications; and a steady series of books and award-winning films and videos for people of all ages and interests.

Recognizing the needs of, as well as the sacrifices and important contributions made by, such diverse groups as educators, physicians, attorneys, crisis pregnancy center staff, and single parents, Focus on the Family offers specific outreaches to uphold and minister to these individuals, too. And it's all done for one purpose, and one purpose only: to encourage and strengthen individuals and families through the life-changing message of Jesus Christ.

•   •   •

For more information about the ministry, or if we can be of help to your family, simply write to Focus on the Family, Colorado Springs, CO 80995 or call 1-800-A-FAMILY (1-800-232-6459). Friends in Canada may write Focus on the Family, P.O. Box 9800, Stn. Terminal, Vancouver, B.C. V6B 4G3, or call 1-800-661-9800. Visit our Web site— www.family.org—to learn more about Focus on the Family or to find out if there is an associate office in your country.

We'd love to hear from you!

Sanctity of Life Resources

from Focus on the Family®

Gianna: Aborted . . . and Lived to Tell About It

A doctor aborted Gianna Jensen, but she survived to tell her story all over the world. She relates the horror she went through during the first hours of her life, as well as the ways God has used her and her story to help others find hope and healing. A great resource for those who are either struggling with an abortion decision or those who regret the decision they made. Paperback.

What Does God Say About Abortion?

This simple booklet doesn't put forth man's words, but God's. Thirteen common questions concerning sanctity of life and abortion are asked, then answered with Scripture. Whether you are struggling with a decision about abortion or desire to stand and proclaim the sanctity of life, you'll find biblical answers here

• • •